THE
CRITICAL
14 YEARS
OF YOUR
PROFESSIONAL
LIFE

Also by Robert L. Dilenschneider

Power and Influence: Mastering the Art of Persuasion
A Briefing for Leaders: Communication as the Ultimate Exercise of Power
On Power

THE
CRITICAL
14 YEARS
OF YOUR
PROFESSIONAL
LIFE

ROBERT L. DILENSCHNEIDER

WITH MARY JANE GENOVA

A BIRCH LANE PRESS BOOK

Published by Carol Publishing Group

A Birch Lane Press Book
Published by Carol Publishing Group
Birch Lane Press is a registered trademark of Carol Communications, Inc.

Editorial, sales and distribution, rights and permissions inquiries should be addressed to Carol Publishing Group, 120 Enterprise Avenue, Secaucus, N.J. 07094

In Canada: Canadian Manda Group, One Atlantic Avenue, Suite 105, Toronto, Ontario, M6K 3E7

Carol Publishing Group books may be purchased in bulk at special discounts for sales promotion, fund-raising, or educational purposes. Special editions can be created to specifications. For details, contact Special Sales Department, Carol Publishing Group, 120 Enterprise Avenue, Secaucus, N.J. 07094.

Manufactured in the United States of America

10 9 8 7 6 5 4 3 2 1

Library of Congress Cataloging-in-Publication Data

Dilenschneider, Robert L.
    The critical 14 years of your professional life / Robert L. Dilenschneider with Mary Jane Genova.
        p.   cm.
    "Birch Lane Press book."
    Includes bibliographical references
    ISBN 1–55972–395–5 (hard)
    1. Success in business.   2. Career development.   3. Self-presentation.   4. Public relations.   I. Genova, Mary Jane.
II. Title.
HF5386.D525   1997
650.1—dc21   97–621
                                                                CIP

*To Jan
who made these 14 years
fun and exciting*

CONTENTS

ACKNOWLEDGMENTS

The Critical 14 Years has been a very different book from those that I'm used to writing.

For example, *The Critical 14 Years* is directed to young people, and its content involves down-in-the-trenches career advice rather than public-relations issues. In addition, I needed to find experts to consult with about subjects I was not expert in, such as entrepreneurship or returning to school. But despite all these challenges, the book did get done—to the satisfaction of the publisher and on time. That's because I received such generous help from people.

I want to thank my wife Jan for having confidence in me when my confidence in myself got a little wobbly. My sons Geoffrey and Peter were most patient and supportive during this entire project, as they were during my other book projects. My agent Reid Boates never let me get away with sloppy thinking, and it was he who helped me formulate the concept of the "14 years." Carol Publishing senior editor Lisa Kaufman helped me to do some of my very best thinking; she knew how to ask the right questions. At the Ferguson Library in Stamford, Connecticut, Irene Delor, reference librarian, took the time to explain what kinds of research would work best for the book. Her fine analytical mind helped give the book added depth. And when it came to retrieving information she really knew how to "dig."

Because so much about this book was new to me it went through many drafts. At The Dilenschneider Group, Joan Avagliano and John Kasic kept that process on track, working long hours and weekends to meet our deadlines. Researcher Joe Barbagallo found information no one else could find. Bob Stone, also of The Dilenschneider Group, conceptualized and coordinated the marketing efforts.

Mary Jane Genova provided a special and heroic effort in making this book possible. She conceptualized, researched, and thoughtfully provoked new areas of focus to give life to the concepts you read here.

Finally, I want to thank all of the young people who candidly told me what they needed in a career guide and who let me know when I was thinking "old." They are a very special generation.

PREFACE

by Sarah E. Moran
born 1973

I graduated from Dickinson College in May 1995 and roughly a week later moved to Manhattan. I had no job, little money, and significant debt from my college loans. I basically had nothing to lose. I found a tiny studio apartment on the Upper East Side with a friend from college and started looking for a job.

I was interested in pursuing a career in public relations, but with the stagnant job market, I thought my opportunities were minimal at best. And then the job came. Bob Dilenschneider, chief executive officer of The Dilenschneider Group, asked me to join his strategic public relations firm on Park Avenue in Manhattan. I was terribly eager to work and knew that this was an opportunity of a lifetime. And then the anxieties came. The man seated in front of me was described as one of the finest strategic thinkers in the business; I knew virtually nothing about public relations or the corporate environment. How would I survive?

From my very first weeks on the job, Bob gave me a lot of responsibility and made every project a learning experience. He also organized an educational program in which staff members and other influential industry leaders briefed us on how public relations, media relations, investor relations, and other areas of communications really work. My coworkers and I were encouraged to sit in on important client meetings, a rarity at other firms. One coworker, Laura, had to do interviews on the radio for one of our clients, and Bob provided the training she needed to do an outstanding job. She has now done many interviews and, with her success and confidence, could train someone else. I personally was extremely fortunate to work closely with Bob on various accounts and projects, ranging from writing sponsorship proposals to advising clients on international funding associations. I learned quickly because I received immediate feedback on my work from Bob. This relationship was intimidating at times, but it was certainly a catalyst for me to learn—and learn fast. Bob expected me to produce first-rate work, so I expected no less from myself.

Based on the fundamentals I learned at The Dilenschneider Group, I've been able to transfer my skills to my new job at a Fortune 500 company. As I told Bob, my experience at The Dilenschneider Group was a better comprehensive education than comparable time at business school. Without it, I would never have understood the politics behind business and realized how to come out ahead.

The Critical 14 Years explains to you how the work environment really operates, whether you have a traditional job or are self-employed.

Bob tells you about the grapevine—the real corporate communications network—and lets you know not only how to protect your image, but also how to enhance or change it. He takes a candid look at the boss and helps you interpret exactly what he or she is really made of. You'll learn how to improve your oral presentation skills. He distinguishes myth from the reality of starting a business and provides advice on finding success in your very first job. He analyzes the politics of corporate culture and is on the money about fitting into it. He covers business etiquette and why it can make or break your career. He gives a realistic perspective on the valid—and invalid—reasons for leaving a job. He assists you in cultivating valuable relationships with the Baby Boomers in the workplace. He tells you about power and influence and why interaction and long-term networking are critical to gaining them. And he gives advice on what to do if you suffer a professional setback. Bob experienced a setback and used it to his advantage; so did Winston Churchill and Bill Clinton.

This book is based on three basic assumptions: that young people in today's workplace are ideally positioned for success in the twenty-first century; that a lack of guidance can short-circuit our potential; and that we only have a limited time period in which to learn what we need to know about the workplace, to thrive within it, and to position ourselves for professional success.

This book should make us feel good about ourselves. You may wonder why, for example, some employers are still cautious about hiring younger people. For many Americans, the post–Baby Boom generation, often called Generation X, seems to represent nothing more than laziness and apathy, as personified by the uninvolved, unmotivated "slacker" of pop culture movies like *Clerks* and *Living in Oblivion*. Of course, older generations have often misperceived younger generations, and eventually the stereotype is forgotten. Nevertheless, we resent the way we've been portrayed, and rightfully so. To prove exactly how motivated this generation is, a 1995 study conducted by Marquette University and the University of Michigan recently concluded that entrepreneurs aged twenty-five to thirty-four created 70 percent of all new businesses and startups. Judging by statistics alone, we are showing more initiative at our young age than any other age group.

Why, then, does the misperception of our collective character still exist? For starters, our attitudes, values, and work ethics are typically quite different from those of our parents, employers, and grand-parents. And on a whole, our views on politics, sex, spirituality, and society may seem foreign to older people, just as their views often seem old-fashioned to us.

In fact, however, our realities and attitudes are powerfully influ-encing individuals, communities, the nation, and the world. Consider how we've impacted the media, advertising, and politics. Nearly every national newspaper, business and trade publication, and televi-sion and radio program (not only those catering specifically to us) runs stories daily on Generation X. Advertising and entertainment execu-tives have dedicated millions of dollars to researching our influences and consumer tendencies in order to tap into our marketing potential and get our attention. Politicians have changed their image on our account, positioning themselves as more "middle of the road" to attract support from a broader base of younger constituents. Dif-ferences in opinion among generations have forced politicians to challenge Social Security and welfare programs.

The environment in which our generation has come of age is vastly different from that of our parents. Obviously, our upbringing has determined to a great extent how we perceive ourselves and our place in business and social relationships. We've grown up with computers, fax machines, cell phones, and e-mail. We have immediate and effortless access to information; typewriters and mail seem pointless and obscure. At the dawn of every new era, concerns arise about the negative implications of the most recent developments in industry and technology. For instance, as the Industrial Revolution changed entirely the nature of European society, offering opportunities to an entirely new bourgeois class, many individuals contested this accessibility, for it was a transfer of power. The moral decay many feel society is experiencing now has been blamed in part on technological advances and the growing impersonality and detachment associated with them. People attribute what they experience as degeneration to technology, partially because they are unfamiliar with these advances and partly out of genuine concern for the future of society. Although all this may seem impersonal to others, it's forever been a part of our lives.

Perhaps because we were the first high-tech generation, we expect instant satisfaction and seek immediate results in other areas of our lives, particularly in the workplace. This trait is probably judged as overzealousness or impatience, but again, it is a generational difference, and should be viewed as such. We want to be appreciated for what we can offer now, without paying the years of dues characteristically demanded by the bureaucratic organization. In his flat-structured organization, Bob Dilenschneider has certainly "broken" the traditional rules of bureaucratic business. In fact, he recently promoted a twenty-eight-year-old man to principal, the youngest ever in the history of the firm.

Our perception of politics is also enormously different from that of our parents, in part because today's media sensationalizes things in a manner vastly different from the more aristocratic, close-to-the-vest days of the Eisenhower or Kennedy administrations, when an unstated agreement existed between government and press about what constituted the nation's best interest and the kind of "news" that wasn't in that interest. Having grown up in the midst of the Vietnam War and the Watergate scandal, we, like other generations now accustomed to the present societal environment, are relatively unfazed by today's parallels, such as Whitewater, the Gulf War, or the Iran-

Contra scandal. This isn't to suggest that we are in any way less concerned with the implications and severity of these and similar issues. We are, however, not naive enough to believe that political corruption, corporate irresponsibility, and racial, gender, or religious tensions are shocking aberrations in an otherwise perfect society.

Corporate America, different now than just ten or twenty years ago, has also powerfully influenced our attitudes about the world today. Having witnessed firsthand our parents' strife in the face of downsizing, layoffs, rising interest rates, exorbitant debts, the devaluation of the dollar and of property, and other general economic insecurity, our generation is less inclined to be loyal to corporations. Bob understands that. Many of our peers would rather risk the possibility of failure in self-employment than endure the uncertainty our parents faced in the age of corporate anorexia. These attitudes will probably change as the next generation enters the workforce or as more corporations institute greater recruiting or tuition reimbursement programs, profit-sharing plans, 401Ks, and other incentives for us. Smaller businesses not in the position to institute these programs are more and more frequently seeking viable alternatives that recognize the accomplishments of younger workers.

The challenges we've already faced are tremendous—divorce, personal debt, the national debt and Social Security challenge, a scary job market— but we've proven to be quite strong in turning adversity into opportunity. It's probably fair to say that our responsibilities are much greater than those of many prior generations, and as such, they have shaped our attitudes to a great extent.

We accept change as the only constant in life and, given our backgrounds, are very adaptable. Bob certainly knows how big a plus that is for us. Sure, we're young and lack in actual experience in the workplace. But when given the responsibility to prove ourselves, we're capable of delivering outstanding performance and offering innovative perspectives. We want to be given the opportunity to excel.

We are capable of shaping and influencing business, government, education, society, and more. To do so, it is important to voice our concerns on pressing issues, through voting, proactive leadership, and keeping ourselves informed via the media and other outlets. In addition, we can educate ourselves, namely by absorbing information at work and elsewhere, and should explore our environments, offering alternative methods of thinking and implementation. And if given direction, we can more quickly and effectively unleash our power. This book will serve as an indispensable tool in assisting readers to identify what goals and direction they're considering, and ultimately to achieve these goals. It's about recognizing individual potential, and using it to the full capacity. The various interviews, including those from a business school dean, the editor in chief of *Inc.* magazine, and Bob's mentor, lend insight into how employers view you and how you can make your assets more attractive. The "Things to Remember" bullets are also good points to keep in mind whether you're embarking on your first career or your fourth.

Bob and I have had our differences in philosophy, but he's always been receptive to my opinion and willing to compromise if he sees my point. Without his direction, I probably wouldn't have been motivated to thoroughly analyze my own perspectives, frustrations and potential as a young person. Until I was asked to write this Preface, I never really considered our generation's position collectively relative to business, society, politics, and the like.

I can't promise this book will bring you overnight success. I can tell you that the guidelines set forth by Bob Dilenschneider in this book can be as invaluable to your career development as they have been to mine.

Good luck!

THE
CRITICAL
14 YEARS
OF YOUR
PROFESSIONAL
LIFE

INTRODUCTION

This chapter is must reading IF:

- You're under thirty-seven years of age
- You're worried about your professional prospects
- You've just had a big success—and don't want to blow it
- Your career is stuck at the minimum wage
- You can't seem to get other people to help you with your career

My office is above Grand Central Station, the transportation hub of New York City. So every weekday I see hopeful young men and women, just like you, get off trains and subways and go to their internships and jobs in New York City. Most are determined and sure of themselves. The poignant fact about this is that some of those young people will make it and some of them won't.

Why some young people will succeed and some won't has very little to do with their family background, what college they attended, their major in college, the honors they received in college, their IQ, the graduate degree they obtained, their athletic skills —or even their ambition and drive.

I can recall a number of young men and women who worked with me in the 1960s who didn't pay attention to learning the ropes. Why? Some had emotional problems. Some were in the wrong organization and the wrong job, and they just shut down and didn't struggle to understand how the game was played. Some were determined to prove that all that mattered was how they did their job. Some were just smart alecks who wanted to do it their way. All of them turned out to be underachievers in the workplace. Despite their backgrounds, brains, and talents, they didn't get anywhere.

To learn the ropes, you have to admit that you don't have all the

3

answers. Every month I interview bright students for internships and jobs. When it's apparent that they think they have all the answers, I don't invite them back for a second interview. I know that they won't try to figure out the infrastructure of our organization—and that they will flounder.

LEARNING THE ROPES

Success in the workplace depends today, as it did when I was a young man, on one thing: learning the ropes about how the work world operates. For example, if you don't understand how the office grapevine operates, you won't know what to do to correct a negative rumor about yourself. Suppose you've never learned to manage your boss. Then how can you get that boss to help you get where you want to go? Or suppose you can't even seem to land that new job or can't make it into business school. Do you know what your next steps should be?

THE BRIGHTEST BOY IN THE CLASS

Roger was the thirty-year-old son of one of my clients. His father asked me to talk with Roger about his unstable job history, and so Roger came to see me.

In college Roger had earned a 3.8 grade point average. Since graduation, though, he had experienced one job defeat after another, ranging from layoffs to being passed over for promotions. He feared that another layoff was coming, and he wondered what he was doing wrong.

As we talked I sensed that Roger was the classic case of the bright achiever in college who had difficulty making the transition to the world of work. Because of his string of successes in academics, he was trying to apply those old success formulas to his jobs.

As in college, Roger would ask provocative questions at work—and would usually irritate his superiors and colleagues. As in college, he reflected a lot on his feelings and current events and sometimes shared those feelings and opinions with coworkers; as a result, his coworkers thought he was weird. As in college, he assumed that his primary responsibility was to do his work well; as a result, he simply ignored office politics. In short, after college Roger hadn't bothered to learn how "to go to work." When I met him, although he had already spent eight years in the workplace, he was still a babe in the woods when it came to knowing what to do day to day on the job.

I gave Roger simple advice: Learn the ropes. Get to know how the workplace operates. Watch what others at work are doing, and figure out why they might be doing that.

I impressed on him that every action in the workplace is functional. I knew that if he came to understand why rituals, procedures, and traditions existed in the workplace he could make a choice. He could choose to stay with the organization and do what he had to do to work within its infrastructure. Or he could decide to find a home in an organization whose values were closer to his. Roger opted to leave.

Now Roger knew that during his first few weeks on his new job he had to figure out the patterns in the organization, or how the place functioned. He turned out to be a quick study. He noticed, for example, that his superiors and coworkers weren't analytical. That told him right away that this was no place to play the smartest boy in the class. Roger recognized relationships there were friendly and warm, so he could chat about his feelings and air his opinions on current events. He discerned that office politics revolved around having access to members of the family who owned the organization. Roger made sure he worked out in the gym next to a family member his own age.

THE 14 YEARS

Normally, the Rogers of the world and you have about fourteen years to learn the ropes. Those 14 years are the most important time in your entire professional career. They are your boot camp. They train you for combat, and you learn how to stay alive in the workplace. You also learn what to do during "peacetime," or when organizational life is proceeding as usual.

In my day those 14 years extended from when we first had an internship or a part-time or full-time job related to our profession until we were in our early thirties. For example, suppose that your dream was to become a buyer at a large store in Manhattan. You lucked out and got a job selling hose at a small store in San Diego when you were sixteen. Well, your 14 years began then, at age sixteen. And for you those 14 years ended when you were thirty.

Some of you will do those 14 years in pieces. Let's say you're going to be a lawyer. Maybe you'll take three years off to get a graduate degree in film or five years to rear a family. Maybe you just want a few years to tour Africa. Your 14 years start when you actually start working in law. That might be during the summer or part-time during the academic year. That's when Work 101 begins for you.

If you don't take full advantage of learning the ropes during those 14 years, you're going to be in trouble. There will be big gaps in your knowledge base, and you won't have developed sound instincts about what to do when, under what circumstances. Without that knowledge base, without those instincts, you wind up what I call "work-illiterate." This was Roger's situation: During his first eight years in jobs, he just wasn't interested in learning the ropes.

Or suppose you intend to make advertising your career. You might go to college for four years, graduate, and get a job in the mailroom of an advertising agency. That's when your 14 years begin—as soon as you enter that mailroom.

FORGIVING TIMES

Why are those 14 years so important to your career? Because that's the time slot in which organizations expect you to focus on figuring out how the whole enchilada operates. During those 14 years organizations will probably be more or less forgiving of your mistakes.

Suppose the team is trying to dazzle a client. You sit there mute. You don't add any value to the discussion. Afterward, your boss will most likely talk to you about it, but probably in an educational rather than a punitive way. He'll explain why everyone on the team has to speak up in meetings with the client. After he goes through his explanation, though, he'll expect you not to make that mistake again. If you do, it will be held against you. It will be embedded in the organizational memory, and you'll start to develop a bad reputation.

AFTER THE 14 YEARS

When that 14-year period ends, you'll be held totally accountable for what you do and say. After those 14 years, you're supposed to know better. And you will know better—if you've been alert to figuring out the infrastructure of the workplace. You'll know when you can go over your boss's head and when you can't. And when you do go over the boss's head, you'll know how to orchestrate it. You won't routinely rehearse before networking. You'll not mistake a bad half year at work for a reason to leave your job.

A GENERATION WITHOUT MENTORS

But there's a big difference between my 14 years and your 14 years. In the 1960s, when I joined a large public relations agency, the world of work was less intense and competitive—and kinder. On Friday afternoon we could joke around and talk about what we were going to do that weekend. We all knew that if the job didn't work out for any of us at this agency, we could go across the street and probably get a better job at another agency. But we also knew that if it did work out, we could stay there until we were ready to retire. Gray hair didn't make you a target for the ax back then. There were no periodic purges of staff.

Most important, back then, there were plenty of people on the commuter train into New York City, in the office, in our networks, and even among our clients who were willing to teach us the ropes. It didn't feel odd at all to turn to the person in the seat next to me on the commuter train and pour out my heart about whether or not I should accept another job offer. Three-fourths of the people, including most bosses, in the office were my unofficial mentors. At professional meetings such as the International Association of Business Communicators, I could always buttonhole people to give me advice on whatever phase of my career I was in. They would even give me their home number so I could contact them in the evening.

All those men and women who taught me the ropes during those critical 14 years had the time to share their wisdom. They weren't working eighteen hours a day in a downsized organization. They weren't trying to be partners in a law firm when there were fewer partner slots. Their boss wasn't fired, or their whole department eliminated, soon after they were hired. So, back in the old days, workers tended to be generous with their time and knowledge. And there was a feeling of caring about the next generation. On the first day on the job, a few people would immediately take you under their wing. Today, of course, you young people are often perceived as a threat. To the incumbents you represent people who will work harder than they for less money. As a result, there aren't too many people in your corner right now. And not too many people are teaching you the ropes, are they? The current workforce is too busy trying to survive.

On a bad day, who can you go to? If I had a bad day at work I could go to just about anyone at the office and "reverse engineer" that day to figure out what went wrong and what I could do about it. I remember the first time the client didn't like my ideas. I was devastated and mortified. When an "elder" at the firm saw me moping around with a long face, he took me aside. He unlocked the mystery of client relations. He told me that dealing with clients wasn't an exercise in building up your own ego. It was letting clients know that your number one reason for existing was to serve them. And serving them meant that if a certain idea didn't work for them, you would come up with thirty more ideas, and thirty more after that until they were satisfied. From that time on my relationships with clients thrived. I surrendered my ego to their needs. For that I have to thank a forty-year old gentleman in my office in the 1960s.

For the first fourteen years of my career with that agency, you might say that I had a flock of guardian angels hovering over me. Oh sure, there would be the person who didn't like me. There were some lazy old geezers who just didn't have the energy to help me. And there were one or two bad apples out to get me and, you bet, they gave me bad advice. But, more or less, I was in a cocoon, protected and cared for.

Learning the ropes in those days was a relatively painless process. And the process worked. By year 14 we were completely socialized to the world of work. I had the system down cold. I could do business in New York City or Moscow, and I knew exactly what to do. I was a "pro."

WHY I WROTE THIS BOOK FOR YOU

Learning the ropes can be equally painless for you. That's why I wrote this book. It substitutes for all those generous men and women who would have helped you in an earlier era. It's the paper version of a mentor. It's boot camp without having to carry a fifty-pound backpack.

This book contains all the lessons you need to know about functioning at work. I analyzed my three decades of experience in the work world. I interviewed experts in the field whose opinions you'll find in this book. I did research. I spoke with you in person and online. You told me that you thought you needed a mentor. You asked me how not to get discouraged when a good job didn't turn up after you pounded the pavement for a year.

MARY JANE GENOVA

I also worked closely with Mary Jane Genova. She's not only an outstanding writer who's done work for chief executive officers around the world, she's a highly analytical thinker. She has the intellectual courage to challenge my ideas. And she's been a loyal friend.

This is the second book we've worked on together. Mary Jane Genova's achievements are numerous. During the Chrysler turn-around she wrote Lee Iacocca's famous opinion-editorial (op-ed) on the level playing field, which was published in the *Washington Post*. Under executive bylines her writing has also appeared in, among other publications, the *New York Times, Vital Speeches of the Day, Chief Executive Speeches, Newsweek, Newsday, Ad Age, American Banker, Harvard Business Review*, on national and local television, and in several books. Op-eds she wrote under her own byline for *The Wall Street Journal* triggered national controversies.

In addition to writing, Mary Jane Genova has, just like many of you, tried a number of careers. She attended Harvard Law School for a while but decided law wasn't for her. She understands what it is to make a career mistake.

CHAPTER BY CHAPTER

Here are some of the specific things you're going to learn from reading and thinking about this book.

Chapter 1: How to size up any organizational culture and determine whether you want to become part of it. Maybe you belong at Microsoft instead of Aetna Insurance, or the United Way instead of the Salvation Army. There are so many different organizational cultures today that there's no excuse for being with an organization that's a bad fit for you. Bad fits are career killers.

Chapter 2: How to present yourself during a job search. That includes what to do about negative information, such as the job you lost two years ago. The best presenters, not necessarily the best qualified, get the job. Hobson Brown Jr., president and chief executive officer of Russell Reynolds Associates, an international search firm, provides wisdom about the job search process.

Chapter 3: Whether you should start your own business. According to George Gendron, editor in chief of *Inc.*, the magazine for small business, there's no one personality type best suited to being an entrepreneur. Gendron explains why and offers nuts-and-bolts advice about learning the ropes as a self-employed person.

Chapter 4: How you can manage any boss in any organization. The boss is never your enemy. There are no "bad bosses." There are only bosses whose needs and wants you haven't yet figured out.

Chapter 5: How to gain access to the office grapevine. Information that comes via the grapevine is vital for you to have. Also, you need to understand how to put information into the grapevine. Remember when the grapevine used to be called "gossip"? Now it's called "survival."

Chapter 6: How to network effectively. Plenty of people are out there exchanging business cards, but most of them aren't getting results. Done right, networking can help you do everything from getting a job or finding a better job to lining up new business or gathering competitive intelligence. Here you learn how to do all this right. Also, Liz Carpenter, who has worked in four presidential administrations, shares her networking experiences.

Chapter 7: How to make allies of Baby Boomers. Baby Boomers hold tremendous power in organizations today, but they often feel negative about your generation. Here you learn to replace those negatives with positives. Baby Boomers are a resource you must use.

Chapter 8: How to develop an appropriate image. Image is your trademark, your signature. Here you learn how to shape it and, when necessary, change it.

Chapter 9: How to have influence. For some of you influence may seem an out-of-date concept. Wrong. With traditional hierarchies coming down, influence—or the art of getting things done—is more important than ever. In many cases, it's even more important than power. Here you'll find out about the wrong and right ways to develop influence.

Chapter 10: What education is all about. So much of a professional life is spent going to school or thinking about going to school. Here you'll look at the purpose of education and its pitfalls. Jack Keane, dean of the Business School at Notre Dame, provides his perceptions on the issues.

Chapter 11: How to balance work and your personal life. The days of the conforming "organization man" are over. You're now responsible for making choices about how much personal time you need and want—and what you're willing to trade off for that. Sheila Wellington, president of Catalyst, looks at this delicate balance and its implications for your career.

Chapter 12: What etiquette you need to know. Since there's been a decline in civility in the workplace, those with good manners are often at a competitive advantage. That's primarily because their working relationships are better than those of their colleagues. The lack of good manners can earn you demerits.

Chapter 13: What to do after a setback. With the volatile economy, we're all encountering more bumps on the road. Here George Daly, dean of New York University's Leonard N. Stern School of Business, discusses how a crushing blow can be turned into an opportunity. I also discuss my own career setback.

Chapter 14: How to find a mentor. I interview my mentor Walter Seifert, former professor at Ohio State University, who describes how he views the mentor relationship. You'll also get concrete advice on what to expect from a mentor, what your responsibilities are in the relationship, and what to do when you outgrow a mentor.

Chapter 15: How to decide if it's time to change jobs. John Johnstone, former chairman and chief executive officer of Olin Corporation, discusses the valid reasons for leaving a job and the right way to say goodbye. This is must reading on a bad day.

YOUR PAYOFF: THE FIVE GOALS

What should you get out of this book? This book should give you the tools you need to be able to accomplish five goals:

SELF-KNOWLEDGE

One, you'll find out who you are. When you know who you are, you will be able to evaluate which organizational cultures fit you. If you find the right fit, you have a shot at being happy—even in these crazy economic times. Self-knowledge is the beginning of happiness in the workplace.

When I looked for my first job, I knew myself well enough to realize that I needed a large playing field. I wasn't going to be happy in a mom-and-pop agency in Rye, New York, or doing freelance work out of a studio apartment in Manhattan. The right fit for me was a large agency where there would be lots of clients, lots of meetings at which I could wear my new suits, and lots of room for getting ahead. I found such a place. Had I not found the right fit, my career might have turned out very differently.

EMPATHY

Two, you'll be more capable of empathy. That is, you'll be better equipped to realize what it feels like to be in another person's shoes—and why that's important. That person might be your boss, colleague, subordinate, supplier, or client. Most mistakes in organizations result from a lack of empathy—the inability to see the world through someone else's eyes.

In discussing success in *Emotional Intelligence*, the bestselling author and psychologist Daniel Goleman stresses the importance of empathy in professional advancement. "People who are empathetic," says Goleman, "are more attuned to the subtle social signals that indicate what others need or want."[1] Those signals help you be on target in your interactions with people.

When I learned to empathize with the pressures my bosses and clients were under, my relationships with them improved 200 percent. If I understood that my bosses and clients were worried about losing their jobs, their sharp tongues could no longer cut me, and I could comprehend the high stakes involved with the project we were working on. So many conflicts in the workplace happen because we are looking inward at ourselves rather than outward at the context we're operating in.

The foundation of empathy is self-knowledge. If you don't understand yourself you can't understand your fellow creatures.

PRESENTING YOURSELF

Three, you'll be able to present yourself effectively: in person, on the phone, online, and on paper. The world of work has always been a world based on image. You were hired, or got promoted, for what you seemed to be, not for who you really were. This is more true than ever today. No one in the workplace has the time to find out who the "true you" is. They will select candidates for promotion based on how you appear to them.

In short, you are your image. Presentation skills allow you to shape that image. Often you only have one chance and a few seconds to present yourself. Just as with product quality, with image you'd better do it right the first time.

RETRIEVING INFORMATION

Four, you should be able to retrieve information about the organization you work for: its products, its players, its competitors, and so on. Sometimes this means knowing how to penetrate the grapevine. Sometimes it means knowing how to read a profit-and-loss statement. Often it requires you to find appropriate outside sources for information about your organization. Those outside sources range from Wall Street security analysts to online information services.

The cliché—this is the Information Age—is true. You'd better know how to obtain information on any subject instantaneously. Some of my best teachers have been reference librarians.

SOLVING PROBLEMS

Five, you will know how to solve any problem you encounter at work. The big players in organizations are rarely the brightest, most energetic, or most creative. They usually have gotten where they are because they have been superior in solving problems—their own and others'. And organizations like problem solvers. It was drummed into me during my first few years of work that I would hang myself if I brought a problem in to my superiors. The only appropriate way to deal with a problem in an organization is to approach it from the point of view of possible solutions.

Often, solving a problem means research. It might mean informally interviewing some information sources. Today, too many careers unravel because of a lack of input from the outside. Too many people still try to solve a problem by themselves.

Perhaps the easiest way to learn problem solving is to observe and analyze how others in the organization solve their problems, particularly the top performers. You can learn a tremendous amount tuition-free. Another way is not to lapse into denial. For example, don't deny the fact that they may downsize your department 45 percent. Rather, admit there's a problem and think about strategies for resolving it. Incidentally, staff members are often judged on how well they handle themselves during a downsizing. A third way is to make an investment in expert advice. If you're confused about your career, and all the other methods of solving the problem haven't worked, it might be wise to consult a career counselor.

A SPECIAL GENERATION

When you accomplish those five goals, you're positioned to soar. You can be more successful than any other generation in America's history.

First of all, you're more pragmatic than any other recent generation. The Baby Boomers, for example, grew up in affluence and entered the work world when the Great American Job Machine was purring. They became too idealistic, not focused enough. Divorce in your family or being a latchkey kid, a tough job market, and a challenging economy have kept your feet on the ground. In the current workplace that's a trait very much in demand.

Second, you know that the only thing to do if given a lemon is to make lemonade. Suppose you got a counter job in a fast-food restaurant. Many of you were resourceful enough to turn that experience into something that you could leverage both at that restaurant and on your resumé for future jobs. Maybe you worked your way into management at the fast-food restaurant. Maybe you got a better job based on that experience. Too often when the Baby Boomers ran into obstacles, they just bellowed in pain. They weren't adept at turning obstacles into opportunities. You are.

Third, you're wizards in high tech. It all comes naturally to you. That's a definite plus to bring to any organization. For example, you can reconfigure how work is done in your department via electronics. Think of the confidence and visibility that would give you.

Fourth, you see through hype. All those hours of watching TV commercials made you discerning. The truck advertised on TV filled the screen. But when you ordered the toy and the postman brought it to the door, the truck was about two inches tall. You learned not to accept things at face value. You can help your organization be appropriately wary of trends and promises of miracles. You can be the voice of reason.

Fifth, you know that money's important. There was a time when some in the workforce forgot that the number one reason we work is for the paycheck, not self-fulfillment. Organizations want you to have a clear sense of your priorities. And your number one reason for being in the workplace is to earn money. You're not a generation that gets bogged down in abstractions about "expressing yourself," "asserting creativity," or "changing the world."

WHEN YOU FINISH READING

After you read this book, you're going to have questions. You might wonder if mentors are more bother than they're worth. Is networking really a have-to? You've seen plenty of ill-mannered colleagues getting promotions. Are manners mandatory?

Those questions are your chance to get talking with one another, parents, Baby Boomers, colleagues at work, subordinates, and even your superiors. **Careers are built on relationships, not expertise.** Focus on relationships, and you'll have access to all the resources you need to get your work done.

Things to Remember

- You have 14 years to learn the ropes.
- Not knowing the ropes puts you at a competitive disadvantage.
- Times have changed, and there are fewer people in today's workplace willing to help you understand how the world of work operates.
- Relationships give you access to the resources you need.

1

GOOD PROFESSIONAL FITS, BAD PROFESSIONAL FITS

This chapter is must reading IF:

- You don't feel comfortable at your organization
- You wonder why certain "types" at your organization keep getting ahead
- You got a job offer, but your instincts say not to take it
- You feel abused at work

My father was a newspaperman. Whenever I run into an ex-newsman in my line of work, I feel immediate rapport. One day, I was at another public relations agency visiting a friend, who brought me in to see John P. John was an old newsman, and my friend knew that I would enjoy meeting him.

Well, John's office was a pigsty. There were piles of everything, from candy wrappers to old copies of the *New York Daily News*. While I certainly did feel rapport, I wondered how John was perceived at the agency and by clients.

After we left John's office, my friend started in on the "Poor Johns" of the world and how John kept getting passed over for promotions. NEWSFLASH: *John makes a bad impression. He doesn't fit in with the buttoned-down organizational culture of the agency. He's never going to get a promotion unless he cleans up his act—literally—or moves on to a more laid-back organization.*

The work world is filled with Poor Johns who just don't seem to fit in with the organizational culture. Years ago, when many organizations were rigid and didn't tolerate individuality, there might have been an excuse for that. But not now. There is a huge variety of organizational cultures among organizations today, from the loose environment of a high-tech startup to the conservative atmosphere of an old-line bank. It's now up to you to find a fit that's right for you. If you wander into the wrong organizational culture you could be shunned, demoted, passed over for promotion, underestimated, underpaid—and even fired. Organizational life never has been kind to misfits, and isn't now.

This chapter is an important one. In it you'll learn about good professional fits and bad professional fits. You'll also find out how to differentiate yourself from your colleagues and stand out in an effective way, even as you fit into the organizational culture.

A HOT TOPIC

Organizational culture is a hot topic right now because we have learned that there's a correlation between a strong or dominant organizational culture and growth in earnings. For example, an eleven-year study by John Kotter and James Keskett found that companies with strong organizational cultures increased revenues by 682 percent over that period versus 166 percent for companies with weaker cultures. And the "strong-culture" companies increased their stock prices 901 percent as opposed to 74 percent.[1]

But organizational culture is also a hot topic for another reason. We now realize that to succeed in an organization, you have to be a good fit with its culture. I remember the days when only tall, white, Anglo-Saxon males could get ahead. We called them "organization men." That era is over. But organizations still recruit and promote certain types of people—people who fit well into their organizational culture. Madonna wouldn't have been able to get a job at Hallmark, but GE's Jack Welch could still have gotten ahead at Citicorp. Specific organizations are interested in specific types. Organization "A" may want a very different type of employee than organization "B."

WHAT IS ORGANIZATIONAL CULTURE?

What exactly is "organizational culture"? In *Transforming Company Culture*, David Drennan says that organizations have personalities and attitudes.[2] Some banks have stodgy personalities. From the beginning, Microsoft has had an "in your face" attitude. Your challenge is to find an organization that fits well with your own personality and attitudes. Unlike when I was starting my career, there's a lot of diversity out there in how organizations operate. It's possible to find a good fit for yourself no matter who you are, what you look like or what you value. So there's no excuse for winding up with a bad fit.

Another way of looking at culture, says Drennan, is analyzing "how things are done around here."[3] That's probably the most useful definition of organizational culture. Everything in an organizational culture—language, values, procedures, rituals, traditions—has an operational function. The coffee breaks at a petroleum company where I was a consultant serve as an opportunity for networking. Free trips to exotic places for salespersons who make their quota deliver a message: *This is the kind of behavior we value at this company*. Humiliating firings deliver a clear message too: *This is behavior we don't want at this organization*.

THE MIRACLE AT CHRYSLER

Let's go back in time to one of the strongest cultures in the history of American organizations. That was the unique culture Lee Iacocca and his turnaround team created in the late 1970s, a culture that helped save a company ready to go belly up. When Iacocca came to Chrysler, the auto company was hemorrhaging red ink. Japanese competition had become a new fact of life. Just down the road was a severe recession that would hurt new car sales badly. At the same time, Chrysler was fighting a public relations battle, trying to tell the nation that the loan guarantees it had received from the U.S. government were justified.

In the late 1970s, most of corporate America was still quite stodgy. Iacocca changed that at Chrysler, and those changes communicated clear messages about the "new" Chrysler. Here are some of the ways Iacocca transformed Chrysler.

- Physically, Chrysler no longer looked like the traditional corporation. To save money, garbage collection was cut back, so garbage was all around. There was no time to file paper, so paper was all around. The carpet in the executive suite was old and worn. All this sent the message that Chrysler was focused on the business, not the cosmetics, of corporate life.

- Iacocca downsized before it became a trend. That told the world, including the government and taxpayers, that Chrysler was serious about getting its cost structure under control.

- Like radicals of the 1960s who staged theater in the streets, the Chrysler turnaround team used drama and entertainment to get their message out to the American public. Iacocca insisted that executives give a certain number of speeches. And those speeches were bold and candid, very unlike the typical corporate speeches at that time. Because Chrysler's approach to presenting itself was so different, the company got plenty of media attention. That helped sell cars.

- The hours were long, and people bragged about that. This work ethic helped Chrysler save money on compensation. To keep its break-even point down, Chrysler had to keep headcount down.

- Many meetings, memos, and other traditional corporate procedures were scrapped. More decisions were made in the hall than in the conference room. This showed the world that Chrysler was serious about cutting costs. It also made employees proud that they were different from all those other complacent companies.

- The pace was fast. This helped communicate the urgency of the situation. It also saved money—since time is money.

Iacocca, a master builder, built an organizational culture that would accomplish what he needed done. Across town, Ford Motor Company established an equally effective organizational culture to support their quality mission.

FITTING IN

The most exciting, most effective organizational culture is irrelevant to your career unless you fit in. That's particularly the case if the culture is strong or dominant. In *Built to Last*, James Collins and Jerry Porras observe that the process of trying to make it in strong cultures is binary: Either you fit in or you are ejected.[4] As I see it, that "either/ or" applies to many cultures today, not just strong ones. Downsizing has eliminated many of the places where bad fits could once hide. As a result, they now stand out—and are generally tormented for being different.

THE ELEMENTS OF ORGANIZATIONAL CULTURE

When you apply for a job, much about the organizational culture is right out there for you to see—and judge. How the receptionist in the main lobby looks, whether the interviewer offers you a beverage, whether human resources seems suspicious: all are clues for decoding the organizational culture.

How do you decide if you'll fit in?

In *Organizational Culture and Leadership*, Edgar Schein presents the eight components of an organizational culture.[5] Let's look at them in terms of you.

1. Patterns of behavior when people interact. These include the language people use and the customs, traditions, and rituals they observe. I went to a large computer company in the 1980s looking for business. I noticed that the people addressed each other very formally and seldom made eye contact. I knew that wasn't the account for me. Would it put you off if your coworkers were excessively guarded?

Customs, traditions, and rituals are very interesting. They tell us a lot about an organization. If the custom is to give all employees stock options, that's a fairly egalitarian company. If the organization still has a tradition of giving turkeys to employees at Christmas, you can assume the organization tends to be paternalistic and old-line. If there are many rituals at an organization celebrating individual initiative, you probably can conclude the culture of the organization is a meritocracy where performance is rewarded.

Rituals are always symbolic. They mean something. I was once on a corporate jet and reached over to get some peanuts from the bar. A hush fell over the room, and I saw the chief executive's administrative assistant turn pale. I looked at the assistant and asked, "Am I doing something wrong?" He said there was a ritual on the plane that no one ate or drank anything before the chief executive officer did. This ritual symbolized the importance of the pecking order to that company. If you didn't like hierarchy, you didn't belong there.

What kind of organization is the best fit for you? There are no perfect fits. Some just work better than others. In New York there are hundreds of different types of public relations agencies. I'd probably be a decent fit in about two of them.

2. Group norms or unwritten values. Organizations usually don't hang up a sign reading THE FOLLOWING STANDARDS AND VALUES ARE WHAT WE'RE ALL ABOUT. Since the rules are primarily *unwritten*, you have to be alert and do the digging. You might, for example, suspect that profits are more important than quality at your organization. Listen to how people talk about those two concepts. Do the two seem mutually exclusive? Maybe your mentor or a trusted ally can answer some questions for you.

3. The espoused or announced values. Sometimes some values are made explicit. These are usually contained in the organization's mission statement or an actual Statement of Values. This is supposed to tell you what the organization is about. At Ford, the official value is "Quality is Job One." That means quality comes *before* profits. At some organizations, diversity is a stated value; that means they tend to hire and promote minorities. Focusing on the organization's values can help you discover its heartbeat.

4. Formal philosophy. This includes the organization's written-down policies and ideologies that determine how the firm will deal with all its constituencies, from stockholders to employees. This will tell you a lot about the organization. For instance, if the organization has declared that it puts shareholder interests before all else, it might do any number of things—such as downsizing yet again or even selling the company—to boost its stock price. Until recently, IBM had a philosophy of not laying off its employees. Because of that policy, security-minded people went to work for IBM even though they might have made more money elsewhere.

5. Climate. If an organization were a restaurant, "climate" would be defined as "ambiance." This includes the physical surroundings and the ways in which people treat one another.

The ambiance in the old-style corporation used to be large,

institutional-type buildings in which you didn't hang up too many Dilbert cartoons. People treated each other with caution. Today, if you want, you can find organizations with warm, friendly, and casual climates. People can be expressive. Friendships spring up easily. And instead of dressing up, people dress down.

I once applied for a job where the receptionist was dressed à la Saks and had the icy look of a model on the cover of *Vogue*. I didn't feel comfortable in that chilly climate.

6. Habits of thinking. At some organizations thinking is done very slowly and carefully. There's no jumping to conclusions, and whatever is decided will be reviewed by committees. At other organizations discussion is lively and employees are ready to take risks. Which one is for you? Problems are solved very differently at the new IBM than they were at the old IBM.

7. Shared meanings. During the Iacocca turnaround at Chrysler everyone, from executives to security guards, shared the reality that tomorrow they could wake up and their jobs might be gone. This aspect of the culture helps people feel a part of something bigger than themselves and their careers. At Disney employees believe that they bring guests happiness. At some colleges and universities the administration believes it is helping to shape the future.

8. Symbolism. That includes everything from the style of architecture chosen for headquarters to how the building is decorated at Christmas. A consumer products company on the East Coast was housed in an ornate building. When the company was acquired, the new parent viewed that building as symbolizing all the excesses in the subsidiary's organizational culture.

Many human elements in an organizational culture can also be interpreted symbolically. If the job interviewer treats you well, that can symbolize the respect the organization has for its human capital.

Whenever I go to visit a new account, I make sure that I see everything symbolically.

YOUR TOP TEN LIST

Many young people tell me they're not sure what they want, so how can they make a decision about their fit with an organizational culture?

The best way to get down to your inner core is to make a list. On that list write the ten—not eleven, ten—things that are most important to you professionally.

Your list might read:

1. A work environment built on trust
2. Interesting work
3. Opportunity to keep learning
4. Respect for the individual
5. Can have good relationships with colleagues
6. Funds to go for my MBA at night
7. Good health insurance for my family
8. Regular raises and a bonus system
9. A boss who's not crazy
10. No more than fifty hours a week of work

This list will quickly exclude many organizations, but it also leaves room for compromise. If the organization you're looking at matches a number of items on the list, you might consider it a suitable place for you to go.

CULTURAL CHANGE

As you change, you'll need a new list. Organizations change, too. Given the importance of organizational culture, many organizations have called in consultants to help them design a culture that helps them work more efficiently and effectively. Thus you might have interviewed at Prudential in 1994 and not liked it, but by 1997 that organization might have transformed its culture.

What should you do if your organization is changing its culture? I say sit tight and keep a low profile. You don't want to be too closely identified with any one faction. You don't know which faction will triumph. Organizational change requires years of work. And the change is not always carried out. The "old" regime might fall out of power and then come back, even stronger. They can undo everything the new regime implemented.

Of all the roles in an organization, one of the most perilous is to be an agent of change. I know a woman who went to what was then called International Harvester. They paid her well to come in and make some rapid changes. Those changes proved too rapid for the organization. She was fired.

STANDING OUT

Yes, it's important to *fit into* an organizational culture. But you must also *stand out*. You must differentiate yourself from all those others competing for raises, interesting work, training opportunities, and promotions. An acquaintance, Bob O., learned that the hard way. He was making a good salary at a radio station, but he wanted more money. He went to his boss and asked for a raise. The boss turned him down. Why? Bob hadn't distinguished himself from all the other voices on the radio. Therefore, as his boss crudely put it, he could hire *another* Bob for less money. Bob had to learn to "add value"—to contribute something unique to the radio station.

No successful person in an organization, whether it's Cardinal O'Connor in the Archdiocese of New York or Bill Smith in my firm, just blends in. In a downsized world, that's the quickest way of getting laid off. If you're not adding value, you're just an expense.

How can you stand out? Find your niche. Maybe it's computers. Maybe it's writing killer speeches for the senior executives. Keep learning. Seize training opportunities. Let people know what you're doing. Ask for honest feedback on whether you're making a significant contribution. If you find out you're not, ask around about how you could be doing something unique. Maybe you need an MBA. Maybe you need to take a few computer classes.

As you add value, make sure some of it is in public. Many computer nerds never get anywhere because they don't *leave* their computers.

Find out what others are doing. Maybe you can help out on their projects. People often get on board with famous projects, such as the Chrysler minivan, just by being in the right place at the right time—and showing some initiative.

RED ALERT: SEXUAL HARASSMENT

I remember the days when women could do very little about sexual harassment. Probably the most help they could get was for someone with power in the office to tell the turkey to back off. However, times are different. Sexual harassment isn't being tolerated now. The law is on the woman's side. Nevertheless, harassers are still out there. When you're investigating an organization, find out if sexual harassment is condoned in the culture. The best sources to ask are former employees. If it is, that says a lot about the culture. I would stay clear of that place—no matter *what* they offered me.

Things to Remember

- Organizational culture has become very important.
- It's not difficult to decode the organizational culture.
- Find out what's important to you professionally.
- Think twice before you accept the role of change agent.
- Differentiate yourself from everyone else in terms of substance, not just style
- Stay clear of organizations that condone sexual harassment.

2

GETTING INSIDE

This chapter on job hunting is must reading IF:

- You're at a pivotal point in your career and you don't know the next step
- You want to find out how the pros—executives earning $100,000 plus—look for and get jobs
- You need to figure out what you might be doing wrong in your own job search
- You don't know how to sell yourself
- You don't know what questions to ask
- And you want to be happy

Each year about 30 million jobs come on the market.[1] Many of those jobs are good jobs; that is, they pay a living wage, offer decent benefits, and seem like they could last more than a few years. One of those good jobs should be yours. And as Martin Yate points out in *Beat the Odds*, "You don't have to be a superstar" to get a good job.[2] "Normal" people get good jobs every day. What these "normal" people excel at is how they present themselves during a job hunt.

PRESENTING YOURSELF

To get a good job you have to present yourself in a way that makes you stand out from the competition. In the advertising world they call it "breaking through the clutter." In your resumé, cover letters, interviewing, and networking, you have to make yourself *memorable*.

Hobson Brown, Jr., president and chief executive officer of the international executive recruiting firm Russell Reynolds Associates, counsels top executives. He makes a distinction between what you *can* and *cannot* control in a job hunt.

"Maybe you're in an industry which is declining," says Brown. "That's something you can't control. But among the things you *can* control is how you present yourself. People who tend to get jobs present themselves as focused, take-charge people on whom a company is able to bet its money. Those who *don't* get jobs tend to come across as uncertain, as lacking in confidence."

THE BAD NEWS

Although getting a job was never easy, it's a lot tougher now. Things started changing in the mid-1980s when America found itself no longer master of the international marketplace. Challenges to our supremacy came from around the globe, particularly from Japan and the developing countries. To cope with this competition, U.S. organizations had to cut costs and increase productivity. At the same time, information technology was eliminating much of the need for middle managers. Thus came the great downsizing trauma. Millions of corporate jobs were eliminated, and that belt-tightening has had ripple effects on many other fields. For example, corporations began to look closely at the fees they were paying to outside law firms; that, in turn, affected everything at these firms from hiring to who made partner when. As business professor Charles Handy observed in *Age of Unreason*, society was turned upside down.[3] And with it went our traditional career paths.

None of us can assume ever again that we'll have a job for life with a GM or an IBM. Neither can we assume that our income will keep increasing, or that our children will be better off than we are. And overtime—plenty of it—is the new business as usual. Many employers are demanding that we put in more "face time"—that is, they want us there at work for longer hours.

THE GOOD NEWS

We're doing better in the United States than they are in many European countries. According to the Bureau of Labor Statistics, the

United States had the best record among the major industrialized nations for decline in unemployment. In 1996, the jobless level stood at 5.6 percent, versus 7 percent in 1986.[4]

Also, your generation seems to be adapting quickly to the new economic realities. For instance, the Law School Admission Council predicted a record 11 percent drop in law school applications in 1995.[5] And it's your generation who would have been filling those seats in law school that once led to a comfortable living but now could lead to joblessness. Instead of following traditional career paths, your generation is willing to try new frontiers. For instance, a list of the successful chefs in the 1990s includes many Generation Xers.[6] And because you're so at home with technology, your generation is certainly dominating many of the high-tech fields such as software development, Website design, and computer animation.

All you need is to get one—just one—of those good jobs. But you want that job to be a good fit with who you are. Remember, we talked about that in chapter one. There really isn't anything called "corporate America" or "the business world" anymore. Instead there is a broad range of organizations that do things their own way. And their way may or may not be the way for you.

When I was at my previous job, I knew a highly competent editor of a yachting magazine named Dean Heine. He was doing well and was great to work with. But he wanted to do even better financially. So he joined our large public relations firm. Dean's performance was excellent, but he wasn't happy. It was a bad fit. After three years, he resigned and went back to his first love. It worked for him. He did—and is still doing—what makes him happy.

Think about your fit with the particular organization and particular job before you accept an offer. Ask yourself these questions:

- Do I like the organization and what it stands for?
- Do I like the people I've met?
- Do I think that they like me?
- Do I know what I will be doing? Is that something I really want to do?
- Will the job lead to something else? What do I have to do to get to that something else?

• Do I feel anxious about the job? Or am I happy to have it?

YOUR RESUMÉ

Before the work world was turned upside down, it was enough when you went looking for a job to have graduated from an Ivy League college. Usually, that gained you automatic access to the best organizations. That's no longer the case. The playing field is now more level. We're seeing more of a meritocracy—that is, organizations are rewarding performance and recognizing those who get results.

Back in the 1980s, it was also okay to create a resumé that was chock full of the facts about your job history. Now a resumé has to do more than give a career history. It has to jump out from the many other resumes replying to the same ad. It has to say, *"I'm* the one to interview." How can you make your resumé jump out? Well, you can't send a form letter. And you can't just rely on personal contacts. What you have to do is *sell* yourself.

There are simple guidelines for that. Let's look at the "Work History" part of the resumé, where you give details about your professional experience. The best way I've seen to organize this part of a resumé is job by job, starting with your current position. First, state the job title, organization, city, state, and the years you spent at that job.

Next, list your duties. Be very specific. If you supervised people, say how many. If you operated equipment, state what kind of equipment it was. If you were part of the product launch team, state how many products were created per year and what the results were.

Third—and this is the most important part—describe your accomplishments. How did your work save time or money, or increase profits or quality? You want to *quantify* your accomplishments. For example, you might have been on the Quality Task Force, which improved quality 30 percent and reduced warranty costs by 15 percent. You might have been on the committee that reduced health-care costs 20 percent. You might have implemented procedures that eliminated 18 percent of paperwork.

Suppose you created a no-frills newsletter that increased employee readership. You should know by how much—that is, a number you can cite. At the time you were implementing this newsletter, you should have surveyed the readers, because numbers talk. But if there are no numbers, you can still describe the accomplishment as "Created a reader-friendly newsletter for 1,000 employees in four locations which increased readership in all locations."

Was your accomplishment a team effort? State that. Put down, "Member of the manufacturing team that produced the first laptop in the United States. Sold two million during the first year."

To come up with a list of accomplishments or results, you may have to go through your day, task by task, and dig to find what impact each of these tasks is having on the bigger picture. Suppose you sort the mail in customer service. Your accuracy could be helping to speed up the resolution of customer problems. Does your department have any numbers on how that turnaround time has been reduced? *If there is an accomplishment in your unit, determine if you had a role in it.* Just ask yourself, "What would have happened had I not sorted the mail correctly?" Connect what you do to the basic functions of the corporation.

Here is a sample entry for the work history.

May 1994–present.	Speechwriter, *General Widget*, Jersey City, New Jersey
Duties:	Research, write, and edit speeches, articles, and reports for senior executives. Liaison with twelve vendors. Responsible for a $50,000 budget.
Accomplishments:	Speeches, articles and letters written for senior executives appeared in twenty national publications ranging during 1995 from *Vital Speeches Of The Day* to the *Wall Street Journal*. Department received one IABC Golden Quill Award and one internal award for quality. Reduced expenses 10 percent.

After your work experience you can have a section labeled "Other Experience" or "Other Skills." Here you can enhance your work record with a description of your volunteer activities. Have you done volunteer work for United Way or the Red Cross? Paula Cholmondeley, a corporate vice president of Owens Corning and president of

Miraflex Fiber Products, was cited by *Fortune* as one of "Tomorrow's CEOs." When I spoke with her, she advised young people to gain leadership skills in the nonprofit sector. Cholmondeley sees nonprofit organizations such as the National Black MBAs and the National Association of Black Accountants as offering the kind of leadership opportunities that might not yet be available to young people within the corporation. In *Management Accounting* Howard Isenberg seconds Cholmondeley, pointing out that "corporations interested in accelerating the education of their most promising managers would do well to look not at the nation's business schools but at... America's nonprofit organizations."[7] Being active in the nonprofit sector provides a tuition-free education. You get responsibility, quickly. If you receive any recognition for community service, such as an award, be sure to add it to your resumé.

The next section of your resumé should contain information about your educational background. If you've gone to college, there is no need to list your high school. Provide the name of the institution, your field of specialization, and the degree or certificate you received. Start out with any program you're now attending. In this section I would also include training; perhaps you've had a two-week seminar in Total Quality Management or attended two Internet workshops. Details like that could help you stand out.

After your education list any awards, publication credits, military experience, and personal information—"married with two children," for example. If you think the information can help you, list it.

Many resumé-writing guides advise you to put an objective on your resumé—a one-sentence statement that describes your next career goal. Hobson Brown advises against this approach; it can limit your options too much. If your resumé states that your objective is to become a media representative, a department that has an opening for a writer probably wouldn't consider you. Usually there are many different types of jobs each of us can do. Instead, Brown recommends including the objective in the cover letter.

No resumé is cast in concrete. As you get feedback from potential employers, make appropriate changes. For example, suppose you listed a job as a part-time tarot card reader, and in the interview you are grilled about it. Maybe you should leave that off. But if an interviewer gets excited about your work on a reengineering task force, you might want to expand your description of that on your resumé.

Pros—those who earn six figures—usually custom-make their resumés for each category of job or each organization. Pros might have one resumé for jobs in internal communications and another for positions in speechwriting. They may describe their experience differently for a large organization than for a small one. What they are trying to do is make themselves, at least on paper, appear to be an excellent fit for whatever job they might apply for.

So learn from the pros. We all have a variety of experience. Depending on the context, some of that experience will be highlighted and some not mentioned in a particular resumé. Be flexible in how you look at your experience. Be prepared to match it to what an organization seems to want.

ATTACHMENTS TO THE RESUMÉ

When I was a young man, I was a man in a hurry. For my first job, I was determined to get an offer from a large public relations firm. How did I make this happen? With attachments to my resumé. I sat down and made two lists. One was the things that I could do uniquely well; sure, I could drive a car, but so could many other people. It was tough to sort out what I assumed only *I* could accomplish. The other list focused on the things that made me different and thus made me someone who could make a difference at the organization. That was also hard: Sure, I went to graduate school, but so did many other people. I limited each list to ten items, clipped the two lists to my resumé—and got the job I wanted. The interviewers complimented me on my initiative. I stood out from all the other applicants.

COVER LETTER

In journalism they call the first paragraph of anything the "grabber." That is, its function is to grab the reader's attention. Your cover letter is your grabber. You want to get the employer's attention. If you don't make a persuasive sales pitch in your cover letter, the employer is unlikely to even look at your resumé.

In the cover letter you highlight the strongest points of your resumé. If you've just completed a cost reduction program that saved the company two million dollars, put that in. Also put in any other recent major accomplishments. (Leave out *less* recent accomplishments, or those that date back to your school days.) Also include significant leadership posts or accomplishments in nonprofit organizations. What you want the reader to say is, "This applicant really has something to offer and is an excellent fit for the job!"

There are books such as *The Adams Cover Letter Almanac* that can guide your writing.[8] But nothing has greater impact than a letter that is in your own voice and is full of your genuine enthusiasm.

THE STRUCTURE OF THE COVER LETTER

The cover letter should be one page long and have roughly five sections (or brief paragraphs).

Section one is where you state *why you are writing*. You want to convey enthusiasm about the prospect of working for this organization or in that particular position. For example:

I'm replying to your ad for a manager of speechwriting at National Widget. I've heard a number of executives from National Widget speak, and I'd like to join the team that produces those terrific speeches.

Another approach might be:

I'm applying for the position of manager of speechwriting with National Widget. I've followed National Widget in the business press for a number of years and would like to be part of such an outstanding organization.

Section two presents your *strongest qualifications for the job*. Highlight your experience and your accomplishments. You don't have to rehash everything that is in the resumé just what would lead the reader to conclude you're an excellent fit for the job. For example, your second paragraph might look like this:

"Currently I am director of internal communications at Global Motors, a downsized organization. In addition to receiving numerous awards for our newsletters, magazines, and video tapes, we've been a model for more than fifty downsized organizations on how to reengineer the internal communications function. Prior to Global Motors I worked in a public relations agency, where my team increased profits by 32 percent. I have an MBA from Harvard Business School and studied in Japan for two years. I speak fluent Japanese.

The third section contains, if appropriate, any *suggestions* for the organization. Here there is a risk, of course. They may already be doing what you suggest or may be offended at the suggestion. However, if you can avoid those two pitfalls, this is a way to differentiate yourself from the competition. For instance, if you're applying to the promotions department at McDonald's, you might make suggestions about how to increase business during the dinner hour.

The fourth section should *demonstrate your knowledge of the organization*. Many libraries have copies of corporate annual reports. Information about companies is also available in the *Business Periodical Index*. Information about nonprofit organizations is available from the *New York Times* and directories such as *The National Directory of Nonprofit Organizations*. Sources of information online ranges from CompuServe to the Dow Jones Retrieval System. Based on your research, explain the reasons you're enthusiastic about joining the organization. For instance, you could write:

> General Widget's accomplishments in new product development are outstanding. Especially impressive is the Widget System 200. I'd like to be part of the General Widget team.

The fifth section is your *request for an interview*. That's the action you want the reader to take. You want him to invite you to come in and meet him. So provide phone and e-mail numbers where he can contact you. Also indicate if this application is confidential. (In reality, though, if you're applying within your own industry, be advised that word will eventually get around.)

INTERVIEW

In the opinion of Roger Ailes—adviser to U.S. presidents, executives, and celebrities—people's impressions about you are formed in the first seven seconds of meeting you.[9] That means that when you go for an interview it's critical how you enter the room, how you make eye contact, and how you shake hands. It's important that you don't sit down until you're invited to do so. Watch the top executives at your organization, or the top officials at your college. Notice how they enter a room and make their presence felt.

During the interview, the interviewer might talk more than you do. That's only appropriate. That person will explain the job to you and tell you how the department is structured. However, that doesn't mean you can't speak up and sell yourself. If you notice that the department has a very busy pace, briefly describe how you worked effectively in a similar situation. If they're launching a newsletter, briefly tell how you were involved in a similar project. If they just cut the department's budget 25 percent, explain how you functioned during budget cuts.

You will also be expected to ask questions demonstrating that you have done research on the organization and understand its mission, services, and products. Before you go for the interview, make sure you have a good feel for what the organization is all about. Although United Way and the Salvation Army are both nonprofit organizations, they have different orientations.

You may be asked questions about things you'd rather not discuss—such as a job you lost or six months of unemployment. The best way to handle those questions, says Hobson Brown, is to be honest. "My father told me that we're all too stupid to lie," explains Brown. "So it's always wiser to tell the truth. If you'll be with an organization for a while, the truth will come out eventually anyway."

This doesn't mean that you have to volunteer information that could be damaging to you. But when you go into an interview, be prepared to discuss the not-so-pleasant aspects of your career. Many organizations have developed ways to find out information about the job candidate—and it's usually *not* by calling your three references! One good way I've seen job candidates handle negative information is to explain what they've learned from the experience. After all, at this point in your career, you *should* be in a learning mode. Tell the interviewer what you've learned from being fired or out of work for half a year.

After the interview, send a follow-up note to all the key players. Be specific. State what you learned about the organization or job and why that was important to you. Thank them for inviting you. After the interview you might win an award or write a speech that is widely quoted in the press. Send a note about this to the appropriate people.

NETWORKING

Studies show that jobs are most often obtained in two ways: by talking with friends and acquaintances, better known as "networking," and by directly approaching employers, which is also a form of networking.[10]

The essence of networking is an attitude. You enter the networking arena with the attitude that you're going to share what you have with others. Networking is a type of bartering. Someone gives you a job lead today; tomorrow, when you're in that job, you'll be in a position to give work or another type of favor to that person. If you don't anticipate that you'll have anything to trade, you don't belong in the network.

When you approach friends and acquaintances, you need to sell them on the idea that you're worth investing in. Therefore, you need to deliver the message that you're highly marketable. This is no place to dwell on your shortcomings.

In approaching employers—"sending unsolicited resumés," as it's called—the best procedure is *not* to ask for a job. Instead, ask for ten minutes of the person's time to talk about the company and your career path. Your objective in sending out letters is to get in to *see* someone. That someone will likely give you the names of *other* people to see. Here is a sample unsolicited resumé application:

Mr. Robert Smith
Director of Internal Communications
Global Motors
Detroit, MI 48233

Dear Mr. Smith:

Congratulations on winning *Business Daily's* annual new product competition. I would like to learn more about how communications operates in Global Motors.

For five years I've been an information specialist at a consumer products company. We handle everything from the employee newsletter to the annual report. I've learned a tremendous amount through this experience. For example, last year I wrote the chairman's letter in the annual report. And this year I'm totally responsible for all speeches made to employees. But now I'm assessing my career and trying to determine what the next step will be.

Could you perhaps give me ten minutes of your time to discuss Global Motors and my career path? I would be happy to meet you before or after normal business hours, as you prefer.

I'll be calling you next week. Meanwhile, you can reach me at (555) 234–5678. Thank you for your time.

Sincerely,

When you do get a good job, don't forget the people who helped or tried to help you. You have a big debt to pay off. Every Christmas, I call forty people who have helped me with my career, even though we may not have talked for a whole year. I fill them in on what's going on in my life and let them know that I still remember how they helped me.

Throughout this book I will present interviews with experts in a variety of fields. I tried to ask these experts questions you would find useful.

The first interview is with Hobson Brown Jr., president and chief executive officer of Russell Reynolds Associates, an international executive recruiting firm.

* * *

HOBSON BROWN JR.

RLD: What's a common mistake people make in a job hunt?

HB: Far too many people think a job search is a very systematic or linear thing. They think you can go down one line and eventually find a job. What you have to do is recognize that you have to put a *lot* of lines out. You may have to pursue a lot of avenues at the same time. If you do things systematically, you could miss out on opportunities. You may have contacted A, B, and C in the beginning of your search and not retraced your steps and contacted them again. And *they* might be the critical link to a good job.

RLD: What kind of mindset or attitude should a job hunter have?

HB: Realistic but positive. You must know that you're undertaking something that's going to take time and is not going to be easy. But you must also be positive in the sense of someone who is confident in their own ability, in their ability to contribute, and in an awareness that there's a place out there for them.

RLD: Any advice on the resumé?

HB: People should be themselves. That's the best tone. And you should refer to specific achievements such as "accomplishing a 20 percent improvement in quality" rather than general statements like "I'm good at achieving my goals." Also, as with the interview, you shouldn't lie to cover over what might be negative information.

RLD: What about the cover letter?

HB: In a cover letter demonstrate that you've done your homework, both on the organization and on yourself. Show that you've researched the organization and concluded that there's *something* in your background that's relevant for them. And don't leave the next step to them. *Say* you're going to take action—that is, call them in a week for an appointment. You have to gain *control* over the process.

RLD: What about the interview?

HB: Here it's good to be direct and not beat about the bush. Let yourself come out. That will make you appear more comfortable. If you're concerned about how the company develops young people, ask about that. Ask about opportunities for advancement. And don't try to impress the interviewer. You don't know that person, so you don't know what would impress him or her.

RLD: There is so much emphasis on networking and directly contacting companies that it seems young people are wasting their time answering ads. Is that true?

HB: No. A job hunter must use every resource to get a job. Ads sometimes lead to good jobs.

RLD: What's the most destructive myth about a job search?

HB: Many believe that "if you're good" you'll get a job quickly. That's not true. Job hunting is an imperfect process, and it might not yield results quickly. Another dangerous myth is that loyalty is dead. The reality is that employers are still looking for people who will be committed to the company.

RLD: What advice would you give young people who have a choice of jobs?

HB: I would advise them to go with the company that has a proven track record in developing young people.

* * *

Things to Remember

- How you present yourself is one of the things you can control in a job search.
- In all aspects of the search, customize your pitch to the particular organization and job.
- Sell yourself through your accomplishments and uniqueness.
- Don't be too linear in your job hunt.
- Don't get down on yourself if you don't succeed right away.

3

ON YOUR OWN

This chapter is must reading IF:

- You want to get beyond the hype about entrepreneurs
- You're thinking about starting a business or buying a franchise
- You wonder if you have the right attitude about self-employment
- You need help starting your business
- And you want to be happy

Have you recently taken one of those quizzes in a magazine or book to find out if you should be an entrepreneur? I'll bet you have. Because of the difficult job situation, many of you are thinking about going out on your own. According to Steven Bursten in *The Bootstrap Entrepreneur*, two-thirds of these bootstrap entrepreneurs are now under the age of forty.[1] Every year since 1986—when downsizing began to rear its head—about 900,000 enterprises have opened or reopened. That's *not* counting the thousands of entrepreneurs who run one-person businesses.[2] You can be among those entrepreneurs.

George Gendron, editor in chief of *Inc.*, the magazine of small business, emphasizes that there is no one personality type that makes for a successful entrepreneur. So forget the quizzes. In his fifteen years at *Inc.*, Gendron has met almost every hugely successful entrepreneur. He observes, "Those entrepreneurs who succeed come in all stripes and all sizes and all ages, all personality types, all backgrounds. Some are very conservative. Some take more risks. I think that there are not any consistently identifiable personality traits that successful entrepreneurs have in common."

I agree with Gendron. When I was thinking of starting my business—The Dilenschneider Group—in 1991, I was probably the last person you would have thought would become an entrepreneur. I had a good track record, but it was a track record compiled within organizations. And I wasn't especially hungry; my career in an organization had made me financially comfortable. Nevertheless I did start my own public relations agency, and it has been successful. That doesn't mean I wasn't scared. I had spent more than twenty years in the corporate cocoon. I had never even had to mail my own letters. But on my very first day as an entrepreneur I immediately became responsible for buying thousands of dollars worth of office equipment.

Like me, you too may be atypical and wind up successful. And, if you are considering taking the plunge, let me tell you: It's okay to be scared.

In this chapter, it is my intention to free you from all the hype that surrounds entrepreneurship. First I'll interview *Inc.* editor in chief George Gendron, who will provide an overview. Then I'll go into the nuts and bolts of entrepreneurship: What are you risking when starting a business? What kind of mindset do you need to survive as an entrepreneur? Where can you get help?

* * *

INTERVIEW: GEORGE GENDRON

RLD: Can you explain this thing called "entrepreneurship" that everyone is talking about?

GG: There are a million different ways to define the word. I guess that the word is very hot right now for two reasons.

One reason is the *classic* definition of entrepreneurship. And that's getting something new done—with the word "new" underlined. And the reason that the word and magazines like *Inc.* have become so hot is that, by now, everyone buys into the argument that the world at large—and the economy in particular—is changing at an accelerating rate. There is a bigger and bigger payoff for companies that can consistently figure out how to get something new done: how to create new products, how to create new services, how to get those products and services to market faster than their competitors, how to constantly change or, to use the buzzword, "reengineer" their processes. And so this notion of getting something new done—which isn't a novel concept, since it's been around hundreds of years—has a sense of urgency attached to it.

The second reason entrepreneurship is hot is that there's a *cultural* aspect to it. I often think that when people talk about entrepreneurship in a cultural context, they're really talking about economic self-sufficiency. They're really talking about an individual's ability to take care of himself or herself economically. And given that downsizing has now become a routine feature of American business, you have a greater and greater part of the population which looks at the world and realizes, as far as the expectations I grew up with—that I was going to get a good education, that I was going to go out and get a job, and that if I performed well there'd be an institution or a business that would take care of me economically—all bets are now off. Each year a larger and larger part of the population is discovering that they have to find ways to take care of themselves economically, that we can no longer count on business, even *big* business, to provide that kind of economic security.

So I think there is both a business *and* cultural connotation to the word "entrepreneurship." And that hasn't been lost on young people growing up. It's had a profound effect on how these young people see the world.

RLD: What are the benefits of being an entrepreneur?

GG: There are a lot of benefits. One of them is economic. You can get rich. This realization, though, isn't new. Back in the 1970s Gerry Goodman and Adam Smith wrote a book called *Supermoney*. The thrust of the book was that the only way to get rich was not to work for a large company but to go out and start your own business. I think more people these days are discovering that's true and are paying more attention to perhaps becoming an entrepreneur. And because of the Internet, there are a lot more small companies going public that were founded by young men and young women. So money is one motive.

However, in my dealings with entrepreneurs I've seen that money isn't really their big motivator. In fact, it's often sixth, seventh, or eighth on the list of reasons of why they start a business. The big motivator, not surprisingly, is control. People primarily start businesses to exercise a kind of control over their lives that they feel they'll never get if they continue to work for someone else. So, I think the biggest benefit of being an entrepreneur is *freedom*—a kind of freedom that a lot of us dream about having. That freedom includes the freedom to make our own decisions, to be accountable to ourselves and to "own" an organizational culture which has our work rules, our dress code, our way of doing business, and our particular system of financial rewards.

RLD: What's the downside to becoming an entrepreneur?

GG: There are two major problems with becoming an entrepreneur, and they are not mentioned enough. The first is that you can fail. We tend to be very glib about failure in this country. But the truth of the matter is that if you go out and you take a second mortgage on your house and you invest your life savings in a business, that business can fail. And the bank will take your house. Unfortunately, all of us in the media—magazine publishers, book publishers, television producers, and newspaper reporters—tend to spend 99 percent of our energy on highlighting entrepreneurial successes. We allot only 1 percent to the failures. But every year, tens of thousands—if not hundreds of thousands—of entrepreneurs fail. We need to pay more attention to this.

The second major problem with becoming an entrepreneur is that very often people—even very successful people—end up with many rewards from their business, but what they don't get from their business is the one thing that they wanted most when they started it. And that's freedom. Entrepreneurs often use an expression—we hear it all the time at *Inc.*—"I don't own my business, my business owns *me*, my *employees* own me, my *customers* own me, my *investors* own me." In entrepreneurship there's a real possibility that the success of the business does not necessarily translate into achieving your personal goals.

RLD: How does an entrepreneur know what kind of business to start?

GG: I think that it was Ernest Hemingway who said to young writers,

"Write about what you know." Hemingway's advice could easily be applied to entrepreneurship: Start a business about something you know. Lots of people assume that they can go into a market they know nothing about and that their business skills are transportable from one part of the marketplace to another. As a result, they believe they can succeed. Frankly, that's not true.

Entrepreneurs must know their business, their markets, their customers, their competitors, and the channels of distribution. There's no substitute for that. So start with something you know. Maybe you have professional experience in the industry, or you've gained experience as a hobbyist. Maybe your knowledge base is from being a consumer. To that knowledge base you want to add some market research.

Another thing entrepreneurs need in order to be successful is character. People who have character tend to be more successful, more often, than people who don't.

RLD: We're hearing a lot about "bootstrapping." What does that mean?

GG: When entrepreneurs "bootstrap" a business, that means they constantly learn to find ways to substitute invention, imagination, and resourcefulness—in other, words human capital—for financial capital. I see this as the best way a young person should start out. Over and over again, we see young people come to *Inc.* with business plans—they haven't actually started a business yet—and the first thing they want to do is go get venture capital. We tell them, "You're nuts. If you're lucky enough to get venture capital, you're going to end up giving away a huge portion of the business. Find a way to start this business on a bootstrap level." We then add that they should think of venture capital only after they've proved that there's a *real* market for this business and they're ready to expand. Right now, the overwhelming majority of businesses in the United States are what we call "bootstrapped businesses."

RLD: Young people are reading a lot about franchises. For example, many of those who bought a McDonald's franchise are now millionaires. What's your opinion of the franchise route?

GG: My own personal opinion on franchises is that I don't see too many advantages in buying one. There's a popular perception out there that, yes, with a franchise you are limiting your upside potential because you don't own the business and you're probably paying royalties, management fees, and a percentage of the gross and the net to the franchisor. But the perception is also that since you are limiting your risk, you're therefore less likely to fail. That's not exactly true. If you take a careful look at the data you see that franchises don't really do a good job of minimizing your risk, and they *do* limit your upside potential. In most cases, this does not represent a sound investment for you.

Most people want to buy a franchise either because (a) they don't think they have a good idea for business or (b) they don't think they have enough management expertise.

Well, let's look at (a). Eighty percent of *Inc.'s* 500 Founders—that is, those who've started the fastest-growing private companies in the United States—described their idea for their business as "ordinary" or "mundane." They attribute their success more to their execution than to the value of the idea. You don't need a great idea to succeed. If you do come up with a really hot idea, people are bound to rip you off and copy you.

As for (b), management experience, most franchisors frequently promise a lot more management support than they deliver. So a lack of management expertise is often as serious a handicap in a franchise as it is in your own business.

However, you may be committed to purchasing a franchise. My advice is that you should be clear and conscious about what you're doing—and what you're trading off.

RLD: How does a young person learn to write a formal business plan?

GG: There are a lot of ways young people can learn to do this. Right now there are plenty of terrific resources. One approach is to go to the library and get a general notion about what's included in a business plan. The other approach is to go to someone who has *done* a business plan. I'd sit with this person and ask, "If I came looking for an investment from you today, what would you want to see in the business plan?" I'd also ask, "Would you be willing to become a mentor to me and help me as I do my business plan?" One of the best-kept secrets in American business is how willing entrepreneurs are to help the next generation out. It is just astonishing. We have a motto here at this magazine and it says, "Just Ask."

Recently I was talking with a young fellow in his twenties who has a very successful business. He also has one of the most astonishing boards of directors. On it are five chief executive officers from the Fortune 500. I asked him, "How did you do it?" He said, "I just asked. I just wrote letters." I asked if he had known them through family connections. He said no. What he did do was send a one-page summary of his business, explain why he admired them and their company, and ask if they would serve on his board. Out of the fifty whom he approached, five said yes.

The best way to do a business plan is to borrow the experience of someone who's been through all that. That'll be simpler than getting too bogged down with books. Too much in the textbooks is overly academic.

RLD: What's better—to take courses in being an entrepreneur, or to just jump in?

GG: Instead of taking courses, I would advise young people to take either—or both—of the following two approaches.

The first approach is to get a job in the industry in which you want to develop a business. Even if it's an entry level job, you'll still learn firsthand about the industry.

The other approach is "Just Ask." Contact every successful local entrepreneur. Talk with them on the phone and in person. What they'll teach you will be better than any course.

RLD: When should a young person give up on a troubled business?

GG: If I could tell you the answer to that, I'd be a rich man. For every answer I'd give, I could find lots of exceptions to the rule. By that, I mean that there are plenty of companies out there which are very successful but which were once on the brink of bankruptcy. Any sane person might have given up, but the entrepreneur didn't. And success came from great adversity.

Personally, I would recommend that someone give up when one of two things happens. The first is when you, in your heart, have lost faith in the enterprise. Not your backers, not employees, not investors, not family, and not friends—but you. If you are convinced it's not going to work, it's time to give up.

The second situation is when the troubled business is destructive to your family. Then it's time to call it quits. At that point, this wonderful quality of entrepreneurs—perseverance—becomes destructive.

RLD: If young people have a failure when they start their own business, should they just throw in the towel on entrepreneurship?

GG: If you look at this year's *Inc.* 500, about half of them had created a company *prior* to starting their *Inc.* 500 company, and half of them had failed. About 25 percent of the most successful entrepreneurs in this country—one in four—have had a prior failure.

* * *

RISKS AND BENEFITS

George Gendron mentioned that businesses *do* fail. In 1994, some 70,000 of them failed. They left $30 billion in unpaid bills and threw thousands of people out of work. There are no infallible formulas in small business, no guarantee that if you do X, Y, and Z you'll succeed.

Why do businesses fail? There are any number of reasons. They include being a casualty of broad economic trends. Or the business may be feeling the impacts of trouble in your industry, competition, or poor management.[3]

There's no getting around it: Starting a business is a risk. You can fail. Because self-employment has become so popular and so prominent in the media, you could forget that no startup, no small business you buy, and no franchise is ever a sure thing.

But as a generation you're well positioned to take the risk of starting a business. For us in the Silent Generation and the Baby Boomers, there was plenty of motivation to go to a big organization, stay there, and then enjoy the pension that came with medical benefits. That option no longer exists for you. Jeff Porten, who is a member of your generation, started an international consulting firm specializing in new media technologies and the Internet. Porten wrote a book about his journey to self-employment called *The Twentysomething Guide to Creative Self-employment.*[4]

On the very first page Porten says that your generation is the "first generation in the history of our culture in which most people think their own lives will not be better than their parents' lives." He goes on to say that the volatile global economy and the lack of good jobs have left many of you in a "constant state of low-level fear, uncertainty, and doubt." For Porten the ticket out was starting his own business.[5]

For you, the upside of self-employment could be tremendous and the opportunity cost low. The upside could be a living wage—plus the freedom to decide how you will work. You might even become rich, like Netscape's Jim Clark. As for opportunity costs, they will probably be minimal for you.

What are "opportunity costs"? They are the returns or revenues you would have received if you had *not* started a business, but instead worked for a GE or an IBM during that time.[6] For instance, let's say you're working full-time for GE. You might be earning $35,000 plus benefits. That might be difficult for you to trade in for *zero* compensation as an entrepreneur. For most of my career, the opportunity cost of starting my own business was very high. In those days salaries were excellent. And that opportunity cost deterred many employees who really wanted to start a business.

That, of course, is not your situation. Your opportunity cost probably isn't significant. You might only be risking a low salary when you decide to start your own business. In my generation, that risk could have been in six figures. Also, because of your youth, you have the stamina to put in the eighteen-hour days. You have the education to do your own market research and then interpret your findings. And, from all your years of watching TV and movies, you have the *imagination* to bootstrap it. That's because you're comfortable thinking on a what-if level. Also, you have a healthy disrespect for doing things the conventional way.

THE ENTREPRENEURIAL MINDSET

How can you know you're doing the right thing in starting a business? After all, your employers might have told you they have big plans for you. You're getting better at job hunting, so one of those $35,000 jobs could become a reality. The economy is doing well and, as in the *Wall Street Journal*, pointed out, some firms are moving from downsizing to expansion. That could mean a nice job for you![7]

Karen Abarbanel has cut through the romanticism of entrepreneurship and provides sobering advice on what the switch from employee to entrepreneur entails. In *How to Succeed on Your Own*, a book geared to women but applicable to all of us, she states—and I heartily agree-" that when we go from paid employment to self-employment we are actually undergoing a change of identity.[8] It's not merely exchanging one gray hat for a newer gray hat. It's opting for a whole new type of hat—or maybe no hat at all.

All of a sudden, for example, you go from being the person giving vendors work to being the vendor asking for work. It's a humbling experience. The world stops treating you with deference, and you can no longer identify yourself socially as part of a brand-name organization like GE or Nabisco. Until your business gets off the ground, your identity is in limbo. And unlike the office—where despite downsizing, bonding still exists—it's pretty lonely out here. That massive identity change took me by surprise. At the time, though, I wanted my own shop enough to get me past the disorientation.

You too can get through the transition if you enter self-employment with the right mindset. According to Abarbanel, that mindset has four major components:[9]

A strong commitment to the business you choose. You don't just decide to sell frozen yogurt because it's a hot fad. By the time you get your business launched, the fad will probably be over. You can guarantee staying power for yourself, through thick and thin, only if you love the business. I love public relations.

The willingness to invest enormous amounts of time. The oldest entrepreneurial joke is that the entrepreneur trades in forty hours a week to work eighty hours. There's just no shortcut around that time demand. Can your family life withstand this pressure?

A strong desire to operate independently. Independence is the heartbeat of entrepreneurship. If you're comfortable working in someone else's organization, you probably don't want to be an entrepreneur. Your freedom has to be more important to you than a regular paycheck.

A realistic, clear-eyed view of the demands involved. One of the demands in many of the businesses we start is that we sell. If you've never sold before, take a part-time sales job and see if you can survive out there. In your own business you'll probably also have to do a lot of paperwork, keep the books, and make tough decisions about whether to retain an unprofitable client and about hiring and firing. As an entrepreneur, you'll have a very diverse job description.

To Abarbanel's four imperatives I would add: **An emotional support system.** Maybe it's your family or friends. Maybe it's your former colleagues. You need them not only to encourage you but to tell you the truth. When I was starting my own shop I had tremendous support. I went to visit my friend Jack Malloy at DuPont. I was riding high. Malloy asked me, "Bob, you've been blessed with a lot of support, but who's supporting your wife?" I got right up from the chair and called my wife back in New York. I apologized to Jan for not supporting her. It was pretty emotional.

HELP FOR THE ENTREPRENEUR

If you do decide to go into business for yourself, there's great flexibility in how you structure your business. You can become a sole proprietor, create a general or limited partnership, or incorporate yourself. As your business changes, you can change the structure. Before you make a decision about the structure of your business, you should read about the advantages and disadvantages of each. Books such as Irving Burstiner's *The Small Business Handbook* are helpful.[10] But they might not be enough. You may have to pay for the expertise of a tax expert and a lawyer.

The good news is that there's a lot of help out there now. In addition to networking with other entrepreneurs, as George Gendron suggests, there are a variety of other resources.

THE SMALL BUSINESS ADMINISTRATION

In *SBA Hotline Answer Book*, Gustave Berle points out that the SBA toll-free hotline (800-827-5722) gets about 250,000 calls a year. Those calls come from entrepreneurs in all phases of their business. They may be just starting out. They may need a guaranteed loan from the SBA to expand the business. Their business may be in trouble. They might want to go public. The first stop for all that can be the SBA. In addition, the SBA could refer you to another federal agency for help.[11]

Along with the Washington, D.C.–based SBA, there are about ninety SBA field offices in various cities across the country. You can get their phone number from calling the SBA hotline or checking the U.S. Government pages of your phone book.

SCORE—the Service Corps of Retired Executives—works closely with the SBA. SCORE provides help to you free of charge. The SBIC—the Small Business Investment Corporation—makes funds available and offers management expertise.

OTHER FEDERAL AGENCIES

There are massive resources within the federal government. In *Free Help From Uncle Sam To Start Your Own Business (or Expand the One You Have)*, William Alarid and Gustav Berle introduce you to some of the services available.[12] If you are online, you can contact the U.S. Business Advisor at http://www.business.gov. This is the new online clearing house for small business.[13]

Help from Uncle Sam may be especially useful if you're considering an import or export business. For example, if you were interested in exporting food, there are the Foreign Agriculture Service (FAS), the FAS Trade Assistance and Promotional Office, the FAS Trade Show Office, and the Department of Agriculture's Market Promotion Program.[14]

THE PUBLIC LIBRARY

If your community library is oriented toward business, you will save money and time. Not only are there books you can check out, but the reference librarian can point you in the right direction to do market research.

HANG IN THERE

If one veteran entrepreneur could give the new entrepreneur one gift, that gift would be the ability to be persistent. There's no substitute for persistence. In a recent profile in *Success* magazine, British entrepreneur Richard Price, who introduced the acclaimed *Upstairs, Downstairs* series to public broadcasting in the United States, attributes his success to "bloody persistence." Price had to make twelve presentations before he could get the series on the air in America.

When it went on to become an institution, Price says, people wondered, "Why the hell didn't anyone think of this before?"[15] Persistence is more important than imagination, capital, and even luck.

Things to Remember

- There is no one personality type that characterizes successful entrepreneurs.
- Your business can fail.
- When considering self-employment, calculate the opportunity cost.
- There's plenty of help out there, including other entrepreneurs and federal agencies.

4

YOU AND YOUR BOSSES

This chapter is must reading IF:

- You're having trouble with the boss
- You have a new boss
- There's an in-crowd in your office and you're not in it
- You realize the boss has tremendous power over you

Most people don't like working with bosses. It's not part of human nature to be "bossed around." Go into any ladies' room, any men's room or any cafeteria in a commercial building, and—if the bosses aren't there—you'll usually get an earful about *someone's* boss.

Industry Week conducted a survey about bosses; less than 40 percent of the respondents thought that their bosses had adequate managerial and personal skills.[1] Columbia University psychologist Harvey Hornstein conducted an eight-year study of abuse by bosses; he found that 90 percent of the American workforce has, at some time, been subject to abusive behavior from the boss.[2] At St. Paul Fire and Marine Insurance Company, a survey was conducted among employees regarding their bosses; one out of three rated their bosses as below par or neutral. Of that one-third, 52 percent suffered from job burnout. Just as interesting, of those who gave their supervisors favorable ratings, only 25 percent suffered from job stress.[3]

A BOSS IS A BOSS IS A BOSS...

If you think your bosses cause you problems, you're not alone. I've had plenty of tough bosses. In fact, I've worked for seven of the ten bosses rated by *Fortune* as the toughest in America. Once I really got to know them, though, they all turned out to be decent human beings.

In most cases, bosses are just human beings under a great deal of pressure. I've never had a "bad"—or evil—boss per se.

In the army, for example, I was an eager beaver. After I finished what I was supposed to be doing, I went to Corporal Nidel and asked, "What can I do now?" The corporal was having none of that. He told me to move all the rocks from one side of a road to the other side. When I finished that, I again asked what I could do. He told me to move the rocks back to their original position. Was Corporal Nidel a sadist? A bad boss? A power-monger? Not at all. The corporal was just a boss with a message to deliver. And that message was "Leave me alone, kid." I got the message.

Some bosses have been downright kind. In a public relations agency where I worked, I was supervised at one period by John O'Connell. O'Connell wrote up a strategy for positioning a client. I read it. I did some thinking. And I told O'Connell that his work "needed to be beefed up." The boss invited me to try my hand at the project. I sat at my typewriter—all we had were trusty Selectrics in those days—for hours, without writing a word. Finally I put something down. I gave it to O'Connell. He thanked me very much. However, he thought it "too sophisticated" for this client, he said. He was going to save it for another type of client. Years later I realized the material I gave him was terrible. I'm glad I had some bosses who allowed me to learn things on my own.

SUCCESSFUL PEOPLE

Successful people, I've found, don't waste their time badmouthing their bosses. There's no percentage in that—and the bosses may find out about what you're saying. (There are moles in almost every organization.) Successful people accept the fact that bosses are a reality in their lives. They don't expect the boss to change. They understand that if they obtain too much power, the boss might not like that. So they manuever themselves away from a power struggle with the boss. They recognize that the boss may have a lot of responsiblity but little authority, and they're helpful with this situation. They're not afraid of the boss and know how to express their concerns diplomatically. They realize that some bosses just want to hang on until retirement, and they refrain from trying to force new perspectives on the boss. In short, successful people excel in the art of *managing their bosses*. There's no boss they can't manage.

UNSUCCESSFUL PEOPLE

Colleagues of mine, such as Bob S., who didn't accept the reality regarding bosses ended up with damn-with-faint-praise recommendations, embarrassing raises, and more stress than the rest of us faced. In addition, often they're the first ones let go in a layoff.

Another colleague, Beth R., thought she could ignore the bosses and just work around them. Bad idea. During her performance review, she was labeled "unmanageable" and put on probation.

EMPOWERMENT AND ALL THAT

You might be thinking: "Yeah, that's how bosses were in your day, Bob, but things have changed."

Have they?

Yes, we're hearing a lot about "empowerment" and "leaderless" teams and a "nonhierarchical workplace." But bosses aren't going away. That's because of the laws of accountability. *Somebody* has to be in charge. It's human nature to look to someone for leadership. When I obtain a new client, the first question I ask is: "Who's in charge?" When I meet the person or persons in charge, *then* I know how to handle the account—because they have the power. Today, they may no longer act like they're the ones in charge. But the change is in the *style* of management. The change is not in the *concept* of power. Even though you might call your bosses "coaches" instead of bosses, they still have awesome power over you. They can fire you. They can promote you. They can make your life miserable.

Companies now hire human resources experts like Matt Weitz to help traditional bosses act more like coaches or facilitators rather than the deities they used to be.[4] But don't kid yourself. No matter how they appear or act, no matter how nonhierarchial they may seem, no matter how much they praise you for your input, bosses are bosses are bosses.

MANAGING THE BOSS—A MUST

In this chapter, let's look at why bosses act the way they do—including driving us up the wall. And then let's see how you can bring these people under control and remember that underneath their bosses' hats they are all just human beings. Great business thinkers such as John Gabarro and John Kotter insist that it's possible to manage the boss.[5] I go a step further. I'm convinced you're putting yourself at serious risk if you *don't* manage the boss. Just like a marketing program, a budget, or the recall of a product, bosses must be managed. If they're not managed properly, someone usually gets smashed—and more often than not it's the employee. You owe it to your career to start thinking about bosses strategically.

PERCEPTION

Often bosses we label "bad" aren't really *"that"* bad. We just *perceive* them as *"that* bad." It's only in hindsight that I have recognized some of my former bosses' strengths, and realized that they weren't out to derail my career. In fact, I seldom even came up on their radar screen. I just wasn't that important. They had bigger game to bag.

I've investigated why underlings frequently see the boss in a negative light, even when the boss is in fact okay. I've talked to employees. I've run online searches. I've read. I've talked to bosses.

One reason we may see bosses as anything from jerks to obstacles in our way, say Fleming Meeks and Dana Wechsler Linden in *Forbes*, is that we want to *be* the boss. The longing to be Number One is probably what got Satan kicked out of heaven and banished to hell. Satan, like so many of us, didn't like having a boss.[6]

Second, the bosses' power over us is usually immense—so immense that we become obsessed with them. As a result, as with any distortion, the way we see them is often not accurate. A mere jerk becomes a monster in our minds. A lazy boss becomes an evil entity who cruelly piles work on us. We also ascribe all kinds of dark motives to bosses who are merely inept.

Third, this is the age of economic *angst*. We have seen three million jobs eliminated in corporate America. Ours could be next. And bosses have a say in whether we stay or go. How *could* you like people like that? It's in our emotional self-interest to demonize them.

REALITIES

In addition to what we perceive, many bosses actually do have problems and can cause us problems. In *Problem Bosses*, Mardy Grothe and Peter Wylie point to eight reasons why:[7]

1. Bosses are ordinary people.
2. Being a boss is a tough job.
3. Bosses have poor role models.
4. Bosses usually don't become bosses because of their ability to manage people.
5. Bosses don't get good training.
6. Bosses aren't good at handling power and authority.
7. Bosses aren't always held accountable by *their* bosses.
8. Bosses don't get the feedback they need from employees.

What Grothe and Wylie are saying is that the person who does our performance review and determines our raises is really an ordinary human being. Thus we should have no greater expectation of that boss than we do of any other person in our life. When you think "boss," think "ordinary"; you'll save yourself some disappointment. Those bosses who are great leaders usually come into your life only once or twice. Not every workplace will have its own version of Jack Welch or Bill Gates.

Being the boss has always been tough. That's because bosses are "sandwiched." Above them are other bosses who can hammer away at them. Below them are subordinates, some of whom are crybabies. Now, in a downsized universe, it's even tougher. Currently, bosses must do more with less. On top of all that, bosses can't act like traditional bosses anymore and chew you out for not doing enough. That must be frustrating for them.

Jeff Olson, editor of *Soundview Executive Book Summaries*, is quoted in *Across the Board* as observing that the best-selling executive business books are those in which the bosses credit their employees—not themselves—for their achievements.[8] The boss of today cannot act like the omnipotent boss of yesterday. We've all read the articles on how bosses of the twenty-first century ought to behave in the nineties. When we go into work we expect them to be just like the bosses in the articles. But when you use such idealistic models, you're setting yourself up for a problem with your actual boss.

Today's bosses face a big problem. And that problem is the question: How should they behave today at work?

For their own role models, bosses often have only their own bosses. This is yet another reason bosses are confused about how to behave. Without clear marching orders, bosses are apt to act strangely once in a while.

Frequently, bosses have no special gift for managing people or projects. They usually rise through the ranks because they are good at performing a certain task—such as selling or writing speeches—yet managing projects and people is what they get promoted to do. Often this is like being shipped to France to run an office and having to speak only French when you don't know a word of the language. Not surprisingly, bosses face tremendous stress in their managerial activities. Most *know* they're doing about a B-minus job.

Many organizations don't train their bosses to be bosses. Most bosses don't even know what mindset to have in being a leader. As a result, they're often preoccupied with themselves and their troubles on the job rather than being 100 percent focused on you, the troops.

Power and authority used to be two major taboo subjects in America. And in many places they still are. So if bosses are unused to handling power and authority, there aren't too many people they can buttonhole to discuss their problems. When was the last time at an interview that the interviewer brought up the words "power" and "authority"?

Many organizations say that people are their most important asset. But bosses are not likely to lose their jobs because they handled subordinates badly. Your bosses know that. That's why they're likely to make so many mistakes supervising you. Who's going to blow the whistle on them? And even if someone does tell, who will care? Few will, so long as the shabby treatment doesn't involve lawsuits.

Up until a few years ago, bosses didn't receive feedback from the troops. That's changing. The advent of "360-degrees" feedback is making bosses aware of their impact on subordinates as well as superiors. This may or may not improve conditions for employees. The benefits 360-degrees feedback can bring depends primarily on how the instrument is used.[9] So don't hold your breath that the bosses are going to have a spiritual awakening and start treating you much, much better. And if you're asked to participate in a 360-degrees evaluation, keep your comments generic. Although those who administer the process claim to maintain strict confidentiality, if you have a concern that is specifically yours—such as family-friendly policies— your bosses may be able to figure out who criticized them for being inflexible.

To Grothe's and Wylie's eight reasons why bosses can be a problem, I would like to add a few of my own.

It's easy for bosses to have role confusion—and thus, in turn, confuse us—because they have the capacity to both punish and reward. They represent both the stick and the carrot. They are both good cop and bad cop. I don't know of too many ordinary human beings who can be comfortable with that role ambiguity. Bosses need our compassion. They're dealing with a new universe, often without a roadmap.

In addition, bosses sometimes don't make much more money than some of their staff do. They know the staff's salaries and bonuses. When the numbers are close to theirs, there is little incentive for them to pull out all stops and do a dynamite job. In that situation, bosses sometimes don't strive for excellence—and that can irk us. After all, many of us assume that our performance is continuously excellent, and we want the boss to be as virtuous as we are. But is our performance *always* that good?

WHO IS THAT MASKED MAN—OR LADY?

I'm convinced that your only option in the workplace is to manage your boss. Any other strategy has dangerous side effects—like getting fired.

The heartbeat of managing your bosses is to find out who they are. I mean this broadly. You need to know:

What are the external and internal pressures on them? Are

their bosses hammering them to meet an impossible deadline? Did
their teenage child just get arrested for using drugs? Have they hit
fifty years of age and fear they will be forced to retire? Let's think of
the bosses in human terms rather than as enemies. In managing the
boss, you *humanize* rather than *demonize*.

What are the bosses' goals? Do your bosses want to become
CEO, or just increase market share 5 percent? Usually bosses have
multiple goals. Try to come up with five goals you think your bosses
have.

What are the bosses' strengths and weaknesses? We all have
them. Usually, our weaknesses outnumber our strengths. When you
do a strengths/weaknesses "audit" of the boss, be prepared for the
weakness column to extend beyond the strengths. Once I got savvy
about the world of bosses, I considered it a major strength that the
executive simply was breathing. The higher you put your standards
for how bosses *should* act, the harder you're going to fall when a
particular boss doesn't measure up. Remember breathing—it's a
major strength.

**What is their career history and their history with the com-
pany?** Are your bosses on the defensive these days or on a roll? We
have become the people we are today in good measure because of our
past. What about your bosses' past? In particular, you need to know
what setbacks they faced. How did your bosses handle adversity?

Anyone who has decision-making power today is bound to suffer a
setback from time to time. You simply can't do things and not have
some of them turn out wrong. Some professions, like financial
services, leave you with more setbacks than others. But a setback can
be a transforming experience—so you'd better know that about your
bosses.

How do they work? Their style of work should become *your* style.
Some bosses read the *Wall Street Journal* on the way in and expect that
you have also read it before *you* come into work. You irk them when
you sit at your desk, on company time, intensely poring over the day's
newspapers. At U.S. Gypsum, when Gene Miller was the chief
financial officer, he would let important information drop while you
were at a coffee bar or boarding a plane. You had to be alert and catch

what he was saying whenever he was saying it. At Bendix, former chief executive officer Bill Agee liked to hold meetings over milk and cookies.

How are your bosses changing? Did one just get a promotion? Is someone going through a divorce? Did another just take out a large mortgage? All of this affects the dynamics between them and you.

MUTUAL DEPENDENCE

Why is it so important that you know who your bosses really are and how they work? As Gabarro and Kotter point out, you and the boss are mutually dependent on each other. Neither of you can get by without the other. Some employees, say Gabarro and Kotter, "refuse to acknowledge that the boss can be severely hurt by their actions and needs cooperation, dependability, and honesty from them."[10] I bet we all know of bosses who got sandbagged by the troops and were forced out of the organization. Yes, bosses have tremendous power over you. But you also have tremendous power over them. Badmouthing bosses on the grapevine is just one way you can do them in.

DIGGING FOR INFORMATION

THE BOSSES

When you have new bosses, your number one job is to find out who these people are, what the pressures on them are, and how they work. The place to begin is the company plan and any other information—internal or external—that states the company's goals, where the company is, and where it wants to go. All this is shaping your bosses' mindset, moods, and goals. You can usually obtain internal information simply by asking for it. I would start by asking the bosses themselves. External information is available online. You can also ask your broker about the company. Read the daily and weekly trade press to keep up with how the company is doing.

The next step is to take the time to learn about your boss in one-to-one meetings. There's no substitute for this. You get to see their body language as well as listen to their words. Admittedly, it's tough to get bosses to give you time, but it's not impossible. At McDonald's, Dick Starman of the public affairs department was having a difficult time getting in to talk with the CEO. Then he had an idea. He booked the seat right next to his boss on a flight to Tokyo. He even paid for his own first-class ticket. That gave Starman twelve hours to find out what the CEO needed from him.

It's up to you to find out where, and when, the bosses might be up for some conversation with you. It may be before meetings—so get there early. It may be at a sports activity, or when they're doing their volunteer work for United Way. Can you be there also? Anyone who whines to me that the bosses are "too busy to see me" hasn't used initiative and imagination.

Another way to find out about the bosses is to ask around. Here, though, you risk word of your questions getting back to them. Often it's easy to get this type of information without consequences if you casually ask the biggest talkers in the organization about the bosses. Just don't be intense.

Be alert for patterns. We all have them, and so do your bosses. Do they prefer to discuss business in formal meetings and just engage in small talk outside meetings? Do they like brief summaries or highly detailed ones? Do they like to see you at your desk after 5 P.M.? Those are the things you need to know if you are going to work effectively and efficiently with them. Write down all the bosses' patterns. Conceptualize how you can be a better fit in their world. For example, if the bosses like short reports, how can you eliminate some of your wordiness?

You can also get a good feel for your bosses by listening carefully to their war stories. If you hear a number of stories about how they and the team were in the office until 9 P.M. Christmas Eve, it's pretty obvious they believe in the work ethic. War stories deliver a very clear message: *This is what I value.*

And nothing changes a situation like change. You've got to monitor your bosses to keep up to date about what's happening in their lives. One change, like a huge mortgage, can change everything. When your bosses take on a big mortgage, they might become more cautious—or even downright risk-averse.

The prerequisite for really knowing your boss is empathy. In his breakthrough book *Emotional Intelligence*, Daniel Goleman defines empathy as the capacity to be able to read others' feelings. That means interpreting everything from their gestures to the tone of their voices to their facial expressions.[11] Our capacity for empathy builds on our own self-knowledge. The better we can read or decode our own feelings, the deeper will be our capacity for empathy. And empathy is the key to success in any organization.

If your bosses belong to the Silent or the Baby Boom Generation, one thing you know about them is that they probably don't know a great deal about all the diversity in the workplace today—including members of Generation X, people of color, and immigrants. It's your job to bring them up to speed on all this. You're their number one resource on social changes in the workplace. You're also their point person for the new media.

YOURSELF

In order to be a true help to your bosses, you must also know yourself. For example, your strength in writing could compensate for your bosses' weakness in that area. Maybe you're brilliant at reading the political winds, and your boss isn't. You can help out. Perhaps your biggest fear is losing your home, and your boss lost a home two years ago. That could make you hostile, or anxious. Know who you are and what you're feeling.

Also, be clear about your goals and values. Maybe the boss wants to make you a double agent in the department, and your values won't let you take on that role. People who know themselves rarely get into ethical hot water.

Self-knowledge shouldn't be any great mystery to you. Start out with a list of the ten things that mean the most to you. And I mean ten, not eleven. That should capture exactly who you are. You might notice that interesting work is more important to you than money. Maybe family is more important than a promotion. Perhaps you find out that you're more ambitious than you thought you were.

Next, make two more lists: your strengths and your weaknesses. Your weaknesses will no longer hurt you if you're aware of them.

Remember, your weaknesses column will probably be longer than your strengths column. Centuries ago, Shakespeare told us that we, even the kings among us, are highly flawed human beings. Often, what makes us successful is understanding, taming, and controlling our weaknesses rather than dazzling folks with our strengths.

To make sure you're not deluding yourself, ask a good friend to check out your three lists and see if they're accurate.

A MATCH

Every day when you go into work, you want to determine—quickly—where there is a match between your bosses' goals, strengths, and weaknesses and yours. If the bosses are pros in marketing and so are you, that's a match. If the bosses are weak in computers and you're a whiz, that's also a match—because it means you can help them out. The more matches there are, the better your relationships with the bosses will be. They need you.

Matches are what count. I've seen very ordinary employees get big promotions simply because they made it their business to be helpful to their bosses. People who make it into the bosses' inner circles are people who help the bosses.

THE RIGHT BOSS

There is this mythical entity called the "right boss." Well, despite all the talk about it, the "right boss" doesn't exist. *You're* the one who makes the fit with the boss right. I've never had a boss I couldn't create matches with. Maybe I didn't like them. Maybe they had a temper. Maybe they sometimes underestimated me. But, boy, could we work together. As a result, I became a "pet" in the department rather than a "pig." The pigs—those who were oblivious to the bosses' needs—were always the first to be blamed for a problem, the first to be laid off, and the last to get perks such as training.

BEWARE OF CHANGES

But situations change. Perhaps the great fit you once had with your bosses has become a little less great. Instead of focusing on increased market share—an arena in which you excel—they've turned to cost reduction, an arena in which you're clueless. You have a number of options:

You can get up to speed on cost reduction. Ask the bosses who you should talk with. Do an online search on cost reduction. Go to the library and take out some books on the topic. Are there courses at the local college on reducing costs? Do organizations such as the Wharton Business School offer seminars? Let your bosses know you are trying to retool. But don't neglect your normal work.

You can also slowly and carefully search for another job within the company or outside. If your bosses find out about your job hunt, have an answer prepared. One valid answer: The new orientation of the department doesn't use your strengths.

If you have been a quick study in other areas that were new to you, you can be a quick study on this too. Your best sources of information are other people. Concentrate on learning the language of this field. Don't blab about how new all this is to you. Bosses don't want to hear about anyone's insecurities. You want to show up for the game ready to play.

WHEN THE BOSS IS FOREIGN

In America, unless your bosses are WASPs, you might say they're from a foreign culture. I've had bosses with roots in every part of the globe. What I always did was learn about each boss's culture. If the bosses were Polish, I'd call up some Polish friends of mine and find out what made that culture tick. Before I'd go to Australia to do business, I'd read the history of that country to find out why Aussies were the way they were. I'd also take the time to learn about the country's customs. After all, I was going to be a guest in their land. When the country I was visiting used a language other than English, I made sure I knew the basics. That showed my host that I was at least trying.

Working well with "foreign" bosses is no different than working with bosses from your own ethnic or racial group. You have to find out what they want to achieve, what their strengths and weaknesses are, and what their work patterns are. Employees who have big problems with bosses from other cultures probably never took the time to learn about those cultures.

Things to Remember

- The boss is the boss.
- You can—and must—manage your boss.
- Humanize, don't demonize, your boss.
- Help the boss out.
- There is no one "right" boss for you.

5

WORKING THE GRAPEVINE

This chapter is must reading IF:

- There's a rumor in the grapevine about you, and you don't know what to do about it
- People seem guarded when you ask questions on the grapevine
- You get plenty of information on the grapevine, but you wonder if all this isn't a little sleazy

Twenty-one percent of those surveyed about their organization's grapevine admitted they "frequently participated."[1] *Twenty-one percent* —that should be more like 98 percent! With all the volatility and uncertainty in professional life, I don't know anyone who *doesn't* work the grapevine these days. That's true in large organizations and smaller ones. The grapevine has become more important than any other source of information, whether it be organizational publications, courses, books, magazines, newspapers, or the evening news.

THE GRAPEVINE = SURVIVAL

The grapevine happens face to face, through e-mail, over the telephone, and, yes, the old-fashioned way—through notes. At one time, probably as recently as the early 1980s, you could ignore it. You could sit at your desk and be oblivious to the breaking news. No more. Now your survival in the workplace—as well as in your own business—depends on how well you're able to work the grapevine.

In this chapter you'll learn what the grapevine consists of, how you can get information from it, how you can plant information in it, and how to "turn around" rumors about yourself or a friend. You'll also find out that, contrary to popular belief about the grapevine, it does have a conscience.

THE POWDER BLUE SUIT

The power of the grapevine first became clear to me when I was working at the Chicago office of a public relations firm and living in Willmette, Illinois. My wife and I had given a dinner party—one we thought was quite successful. But the talk on the commuter train the next morning was not about the success of the party. It was about one of the guests. He had worn a powder blue suit, when the rest of us were wearing dark suits. By 9 A.M., just about every professional working in Chicago knew about the suit caper. That man's ability to conduct business in the Chicago area was finished. Could he have recovered from this? You bet. But either he didn't know how or he didn't ask anyone's help. And he faded from the scene. After that, I clearly saw that the grapevine was not just a rumor mill. It helped to determine who was fit to do business in town. Like God, it made judgments.

THIS THING CALLED "THE GRAPEVINE"

In *Corporate Cultures*, Terrence Deal and Allan Kennedy call the grapevine the "cultural network." This network is the primary means of communications within an organization and, unlike all the other functions in that organization, it operates with no regard to rank or status.[2] The grapevine is a very democratic institution. Those with access to power—and therefore information—have a lot of clout on the grapevine. They include administrative assistants, secretaries, and executive assistants. To get in, all you need is for them to like you—and trust you.

The grapevine works very quickly. Keith Davis did a study of the grapevine in a manufacturing company. At eleven o'clock one evening, a manager's wife had a baby at the local hospital. By two the next afternoon, some 46 percent of the company's employees knew about the birth.[3]

Messages travel the grapevine in the form of headlines. Gordon Allport, the well-known psychologist, wrote in *The Psychology of Rumor:* "As a rumor travels, it tends to grow shorter, more concise, more easily grasped and told."[4] A message may start out as "Kramer unfairly fired by headquarters." But soon it will travel as "Kramer canned."

STARTING OUT

If you're alert, likeable, and willing to invest some time, you can learn to work any grapevine in any organization. There are professionals, like media relations person Richard Kosmicki, who are geniuses at connecting with the right people at the right time and getting their trust. As a result, Kosmicki has an excellent track record of pairing up the right reporter at the right publication or television show with his client, at just the right time. All this goes back to Kosmicki's own days as a newspaper reporter, when he learned to tap into the grapevine for his stories.

Maybe you won't become a Kosmicki, but you can do well enough on the grapevine to protect your job and advance your career. You may be new at your job or at running a business. Let's see how you access the grapevines you need.

NEW AT WORK

Being new at something is a little overwhelming. You may want to hide during those first few weeks. Bad move.

If people at your organization are going to pass along information to you, they have to know you. They have to know you can be trusted and will "protect your sources"—that is, not reveal the name of the person who gave you the information. Therefore you should be accessible. If coworkers come to your door, stop what you're doing, stand up, and talk to them. If you have the time, invite them to take a seat. Or make a lunch appointment. But this shouldn't be your only entree to the grapevine. Search out *sub*-grapevines, those that feed into and carry material out of the main grapevine. Maybe this sub-grapevine is the weekly Weight Watchers meeting at the company. Maybe it's all those employees with preteens at the Country Day

School. Or it could be everyone who's going to school at night. Because people in such groups come from all parts of the organization, they become pools full of information.

You should also connect with grapevines in other departments, not just your own. Suppose you do business with the finance department. After a while, if they get to know you, they'll share information with you about what's going on there. Another type of grapevine would be social circles you don't normally travel in. Make an effort to be friends with people at work who are *not* the kind of people you would normally socialize with. Invite them to lunch or to golf on Saturday. If you restrict yourself to people just like yourself, you'll wind up restricting the kind of information you get access to.

It pays to be tolerant on a grapevine. We normally make judgments about others. This could work against you on the grapevine. Suppose you take an instant dislike to Peter Jones from the mailroom because he talks too much. Well, Jones may be an excellent source of information. Someday Jones may be your champion and tell everybody about the long hours you put in. There's simply no percentage in being critical of people on the grapevine. There's also the Principle of Reciprocity. If you dislike someone, that person is bound to dislike you. And then you lose a contact on the grapevine.

SELF-EMPLOYMENT

Working for yourself doesn't free you from needing to seek out information on the grapevine. In fact, because you're more or less alone out there, you need information *more* than an employee does. And you need it from all sorts of grapevines. You will need to penetrate the grapevine at all your clients' shops. You will need to find out what's really going on throughout your industry. And you will need to know what other entrepreneurs in the community are doing. Are those entrepreneurs as slow in getting orders as you, or are you doing something wrong in your business? Then there are the suppliers in your industry. Because they live or die based on the orders they receive, they usually have a good feel for what's happening.

Since you are the one marketing your services—the person asking for the orders—you usually have less power than your client. Therefore, when you go to the client's organization, you have to be careful how you penetrate the grapevine there. Some clients like to keep vendors on a short leash and don't want you talking to others in the organization. If so, you'll have to respect that. Never wander around an organization unless you know your client would approve of it. In many client-vendor relationships, the grapevine turns out to be one person: your client. And that client is not likely to share information with you if you ask questions too intensely.

Another way to penetrate the grapevines of client organizations, supplier groups, and entrepreneurs is to join the professional groups those people belong to. You may come away with not only information but also new business.

I've found that the dumbest mistake self-employed people can make is to assume they are *part* of the clients' organizations and get too comfortable. For example, they start broadcasting information from the client's organization, and someone in the organization finds out about it. Then there's trouble. It's wise to always consider yourself an outsider, no matter how good relations are.

WHAT DOES IT ALL MEAN?

Information usually comes from the grapevine in a pretty raw state. Let's go back to that grapevine message, "Kramer canned." No one has bothered interpreting in detail what Kramer's firing could mean to you. No one may have thought through how Kramer's firing will affect your department or the organization in general. To dig down to what it all means, you may have to consult what I like to call the "Greek Chorus." All types of people belong to the Greek Chorus of a company. What all these people have in common is enough time at the company to have a unique perspective, wisdom about organizational machinations, no ax to grind, and discretion. Just as in the Greek dramas of old, the organization's Greek Chorus will usually articulate the truth of the situation. The Chorus may interpret "Kramer canned" in any number of ways:

- A precedent has been set, since no one has been fired at General Manufacturing since 1975.

- Management is attempting to get a message out: *No one is indispensable.*

- The door is open to younger people now breaking into senior management—if they want to go after Kramer's job.
- Headquarters is now all-powerful, and the authority of the subsidiaries has been greatly weakened.

If you want the realities behind the headlines, make friends with at least one member of the Greek Chorus. You will know who they are: Everyone respects them and their judgment. One way to make friends is to bring them information they may not have access to. Approach the giving of information casually: "Oh, by the way, did you hear...."

GETTING ZAPPED

Believe me, it's happened to all of us. Something we've confided to just a few people gets all around the organization. You said you were sorry that Kramer got fired, but it's traveling the grapevine that you're *not* sorry Kramer got fired—and people want to know what you have against Kramer. You only told one person you were job hunting—and you're *sure* it's not that person who's the leak—but this morning your boss asked you why you're looking for another job.

Why do these things happen, and what can you do about it? You get zapped for a number of reasons, all of them curable.

Perhaps you trusted too quickly. Remember, *everyone* in an organization has an agenda. And someone's agenda may involve squashing you, or getting dirt from your department and passing it on.

Or maybe you shared your feelings too freely. Work isn't your Wednesday night support group. You can't expect everyone at work to be on the lookout for your interests. Your coworkers not only couldn't care less, they could use the material against you.

There are creatures in any organization who excel in the art of pumping other employees for information and passing it on. They include:

The Good Mother. These poisonous entities prey on young people who are either new to an organization or in a crisis. On the surface, they are warm and caring. They use a concerned tone when they speak with you. They seem sympathetic as they probe for information, saying things like "It must be difficult to work for a controller like Maxine" or "You must be getting pretty burned out by all that overtime." Be friendly with these people, but say nothing you wouldn't announce over the loudspeaker.

Moles. Ask who the moles are. These insecure creeps believe the only way they can survive in an organization is to bring dirt back to the boss. They will take you to lunch and ask about every aspect of your job. It's politically astute to go to lunch with them if they ask you to, but focus only on positive things about your job. If you don't reveal something negative, they'll get visibly frustrated. Eventually they'll stop pumping you.

The Embittered. They have an ax to grind. Maybe they were passed over for a promotion because they didn't have an MBA. Maybe the person who brought them into the organization was fired. Maybe they perceive that others are getting more travel opportunities than they are. So they try to create havoc at work. They do this by plugging misleading information into the grapevine. If they find a reason to dislike you or resent you, you could be a victim. The good news is that it's easy to spot those troublemakers: They're the ones with the visible chips on their shoulders. The bad news is that you might have to do some damage control if they make you a target.

DAMAGE CONTROL

There's a misleading rumor in the grapevine, and this time it's about you. What do you do? Well, the worst thing to do is to do nothing. Your silence reinforces the credibility of the rumor.

The best approach is to involve intermediaries. Get other people to do your dirty work. The simple fact that they're standing up for you will look good. Also, they can help replace the rumor with the truth. Often these intermediaries will be your friends at work. Other times mere acquaintances will be willing to go to bat for you. Maybe they dislike your enemy. Maybe this happened to them before. Maybe they think you got a raw deal. Whatever their reasons, if they help you, thank them. You owe them big time.

You can also fight back on your own. Go to the biggest talkers in the organization and tell them that you heard a rumor about you and, since it contained wrong information, you'd like to clear up the misunderstanding. Then tell your version of the story. Be calm; the calmer you are, the more credible you'll seem. Simply tell them the facts. Try not to place blame. Blaming someone will get you involved in a battle. All you want to do is get the facts straight.

GETTING BACK ON YOUR FEET

In this erratic brave new world of professional life, more people are getting into the grapevine soup more and more often. Maybe they didn't make their quota this quarter. Maybe the whole department is in trouble for going over budget. Maybe they were passed over for a promotion. They're embarrassed. They figure everyone is talking about them. And probably everyone is.

If this happens to you, what should you do? Well, there's truth to the old saying that the biggest part of success is just showing up. And it's especially true when you've had a reversal. In western Pennsylvania, a state senator's administrative assistant ran for local office and lost. She didn't come in to work the next day. The grapevine had a field day talking about her lack of courage. And she never recovered. So, first of all, show up.

Second, if you were wrong, or if you're responsible for what went wrong, admit it publicly. There's no need to overdo this and confess your sins to the world. Just admit what happened. For example, a writer was abrupt with a secretary. The secretary told everyone in the office about this. The writer told the biggest talkers in the organization how she had been abrupt and regretted it. She didn't, however, go into an explanation of her tendency to be impatient. Say enough but not too much.

Third, insert your upcoming plans into the grapevine. That will get the organization to look at your future rather than your past. Mention your plans, to cite one possible example, on how you intend to make your quota.

YOUR CHAMPIONS

If you get lucky, someone—or perhaps several people—in the organization may be your champion on the grapevine. This happened at an auto company to a young woman who had just moved to the Midwest from New York. A director was attracted to her brashness.

He praised her in meetings. Although she was new, her reputation for being an outstanding strategic thinker spread quickly.

To attract champions, try to be where executives are. Volunteer for task forces, even if they're for corny things like the fiftieth anniversary of the company. Or try to "adopt" a champion. If you speak well of Bert, he'll speak well of you. The arrangement is most effective if you're not known to be friends.

YOUR VALUES

The grapevine isn't amoral. Keith Davis tells the story of executives who weren't invited to a company social function. Most of the executives who weren't invited never heard about the party.[5] That is, those who participate in the grapevine often have scruples. They hestitate to reveal directly information which would hurt someone.

But that isn't to say the grapevine can't get nasty. At the organization formerly called International Harvester, a strike was going on. Bonus time came for the executives. Chief executive officer Archie McCartle was advised not to take a large bonus, at least not when the strikers were suffering. McCartle ignored the advice. On the grapevine, he came to represent the bad guy. Eventually he lost his job. He became a casualty of his own greed—and of the grapevine.

If you want to feel good about yourself during the day and be able to sleep at night, you will need to develop a set of values for dealing with the grapevine. You have to establish the rules for yourself. When I was in my first job, I knew that I had to write down the grapevine rules I would follow. I follow those same rules today. They are:

- If anyone begins a negative discussion about a friend of mine, I promptly inform them that the person is a friend and I'm not comfortable discussing this. Sometimes I add positive information about my friend.

- If negative information comes my way about someone—even an enemy—and I know it's not true, I set the record straight. And I hope that someone will do the same for me.

- If I hear there's erroneous information out there about me, I try to track down the source. If I can't find the source, I still fight back, using both intermediaries and my own direct input.

- I always help people new to the organization adjust to the grapevine.

You can create rules for yourself. The list needn't be long. You *can* control your relationship with the grapevine.

Things to Remember

- The grapevine is a must in professional life.
- Anyone can learn to work the grapevine.
- Don't trust too easily.
- If attacked, fight back.
- Create your own code of conduct for dealing with the grapevine.

6

NETWORKING

This chapter is must reading IF:

- You want a better job
- You need more information about what's going on in your organization and field of expertise
- You want to get support from others
- You feel all alone

Over and over again, networking has proved to be a dynamite tool for finding jobs, lobbying for a promotion, lining up new business, finding out what's going on in your organization, getting competitive intelligence about your industry, brainstorming about solutions for problems, creating a support group, and being of service to other people.

You can network on the Internet, on the phone, on the 6:02 A.M. commuter train to Manhattan, in the cafeteria at work, in associations, in clubs, at church, in your condo's laundromat, in the supermarket, at trade shows, on elevators, in rest rooms, on the line to see the movie, at your daughter's dance recital, and just about anywhere people are. In essence, all networking is is reaching out to another person.

MASTER NETWORKERS

One master networker and multitalented man is John Kao, who has an MBA from Harvard and a Ph.D. in psychiatry from Yale. He teaches at Harvard Business School and was the executive producer of the movie *sex, lies, and videotape*. As the *Economist* points out, Kao's networking genius is that he can bring different worlds together. For instance, he can bring Harvard and Yale together as well as the worlds of business and psychology. His Rolodex has 4,000 entries. But it's the quality of those entries that counts, not the quantity.[1] One advantage of networking that's often overlooked is that it allows you, just like Kao, to experience diverse points of view. That means if you're working in steel you can probably get unique perspectives about the steel industry if you network with those in the electronics or consumer products industries.

Another master networker is President Bill Clinton, who has been called the "networking president." In the *Futurist*, Jessica Lipnack and Jeffrey Stamps, who were at Oxford when Clinton was there, report that even back then he was networking. When he met people he would put their names in a little black book with some relevant details. He wanted to make sure he wouldn't forget them. When he became president, Clinton, like Kao, could also bring diverse worlds together, ranging from politics to high technology.[2]

Another top pro in networking is Liz Carpenter. She was Vice President Lyndon B. Johnson's executive assistant in 1961 and in 1963 became press secretary and staff director for the first lady. In addition, she was appointed by Gerald Ford as an International Women's Year commissioner and by Jimmy Carter as assistant secretary of the new Department of Education. President Clinton named her to his advisory committee for the White House Conference on Aging. She writes and lectures and is a frequent commentator on the political scene.

* * *

INTERVIEW: LIZ CARPENTER

RLD: What's this thing we call "networking"?

LC: Networking is standing on the shoulders of others to help you get where you want to go. It's people helping each other.

RLD: When did you become first involved in networking?

LC: In 1971 I was one of 271 women who founded the National Women's Political Caucus. What we wanted to do was what men had been doing for a long time, and that's the buddy system. The buddy system gave men access and power. For example, the buddies who had attended A&M College in Texas would share among themselves their knowledge of job openings, while the world at large might never find out that such-and-such a position was open. You saw the same kind of dynamics in the "old frat" buddy system. In that system fraternity brothers helped each other long after they were off campus and in business.

Well, we in the National Women's Caucus decided we could get that same access and power. We learned networking in a hurry. And we became good at it. For example, we helped get Ann Richards elected governor of Texas.

Initially we eased our way in. We watched for job vacancies. The Carter administration was very friendly to women, and we made progress. But when Carter lost the election, we had to move quickly to find jobs for ourselves. We were constantly phoning each other and helping each other write resumés in a nontrite way.

RLD: You said you learned how to network in a hurry. What did you learn?

LC: Well, at the top of the list of what you learn is to give a hand to someone who needs help. We also learned not to be intimidated by political male animals. We realized that they were watching us, and we learned to talk back.

RLD: You worked in the Johnson administration. How did LBJ use networking?

LC: LBJ handled networking as if it were a symphony and he was the orchestra leader. He had started out in Washington, D.C., as an elevator boy, became an assistant to a congressman, then ran for office. He knew where to go to get things done. It was LBJ's networking skills which got civil rights legislation passed. Here was a case of someone who used power to accomplish good. It's too bad so many people have a negative notion of power.

RLD: Was politics ahead of business in using networking as a tool?

LC: No, Bob, business always knew the value of networking.

RLD: You make networking sound philanthropic—people helping people. Do you mean that?

LC: Yes, I do. But not everyone does. There are those in networks who are selfish and greedy and, as the saying goes, "take the money and run." Despite the existence of those types of people, I look upon networking as sharing goodwill.

RLD: In networking I call the exchange of favors the "favor bank." What do you do if someone doesn't reciprocate—that is, the person doesn't return a favor?

LC: I remember.

RLD: What kind of mistakes can you make in networking?

LC: You might recommend someone for a job and it doesn't work out. When that happens the best thing is to "sweep it under the rug" and move on.

RLD: What would you advise young people to do to form a network?

LC: They can start off with a circle of friends. These will be the people they go through life with. LBJ gave friendship and got it.

* * *

THE RIGHT ATTITUDE

From what Liz Carpenter says about networking, I think you can see that networking is an attitude. That attitude says: *I want to be of help to someone who needs it.* That's why too many people get nothing substantial from networking. They have an attitude, but the wrong one. They believe that their welfare is the only thing that really matters, and they take little interest in the needs of others on the network. They are the kind whom Liz Carpenter calls "selfish and greedy."

Bob H. was one of those. He was on the phone every evening talking to those of us public relations people based in Manhattan about how we could help him get a job. We helped him with his resumé and cover letter. We coached him in how to present himself in interviews. After interviews we led him through the postmortem on how it went. Well, Bob H. did get a job. And we never heard from Bob H. until he was out of work again. We wrote him off as a bad debt.

When you reach out you have to be prepared both to receive, and to give. Networking is one of mankind's oldest bartering systems. If I help you get a job, you'll help me get my mother into a nursing home. If you coach me on how to ask for a raise, I'll share my fishing secrets with you. If you'll listen to me whine about my boss, I'll listen to you whine about your boss. The core of networking is give and take.

In a year some of us build up a large debt on the network. Sometimes we have to be creative in how to repay that debt. One man gives lavish parties and pays off the debt that way. One woman gives expensive gifts at Christmas. I usually like to pay off my debt by doing a favor for someone.

HOW NETWORKING OPERATES

Networking has its own rules. You have to know them. Here's how you should operate.

Create headlines. Just as it does on the grapevine, information travels networks in the form of headlines. "Joe out of work—again." "Marcia retooling herself." "Jan in carpet-cleaning business." "Paul offering new investment vehicles." "Frank has new job." Diane Cole and Loraine Calvacca advise networkers to be proactive and to prepare their own headlines. Don't leave it to the group to create a headline for you. "To get your name on everyone's lips," they say, "decide on the message—call it a headline—you want to convey."[3]

Before you go someplace to network, first figure out what a useful headline would be for you. If you're changing careers from teaching to sales, your headline shouldn't be "Marsha award-winning teacher." That locks you into the past. An appropriate headline would be "Marsha interested in sales." If your situation changes—say you switch from looking for a job to opening your own business—you would also change your headline. Practice saying your headline before you actually network. It should be short—twenty seconds maximum.

Look at the long term. The worst way to start networking is this one: You find yourself out of a job, you scan the newspaper for networking groups, and you make a commitment to yourself to go to all of them for a month. That simply won't work. The best time to join a network is when things are going great.

Just like investing in the stock market, networking is a long-term activity. You can't just parachute into a group and expect all kinds of results. People don't know you. You haven't helped anyone. You haven't given service on behalf of a group. All of those are necessary in networking.

There are rarely quick hits in networking. Ellen Volpe, president of American Business Associates of Long Island, observes that "networking is not selling." You don't look for an order but rather for a relationship.[4]

That's why it's offputting to have a new group member methodically survey the room and target the people that are "must-talks." Again, this is not sales. You're not there to get an order. You're there to develop relationships over time. Those relationships lead you to other people you ought to know. Fifty-something executives have a strong network in many organizations, because they have had years to establish and strengthen relationships. When you join that organization and network, don't expect great results right away.

Keep work networks separate from outside networks. In *Management Review*, Andrew Olson shrewdly observed that it's wise to keep the office separate from the outside. The reasons are, Olson says, "to ensure confidentiality and provide a broader perspective."[5]

That means that you need two kinds of networks—the kind you find in the office and the kind you find in the community. In an outside network you're bound to get more support. You can't expect that inside your organization. Even though there's a lot of rhetoric about teamwork, when a promotion comes up, only one person gets it.

Do your homework before you go to the group. If I'm going to a general gathering, I make sure that I hear the news beforehand. The national and local news is something I should know, and it's a good icebreaker. If I'm having lunch with a judge, I first do a literature search about judicial matters. This enables me to ask intelligent questions.

Mickey Veich points out that networking is more than looking good and passing out business cards. "Asking questions is very important, especially the right ones," says Veich. He adds that doing your homework, so that you can ask the right questions, can make or break your networking efforts.[6]

Volunteer. There are two types of service. One type is helping out individuals. The other type is helping out the organization. Both will enhance your reputation in the group. Also, by working with other members you greatly expand your network. That's because those members may introduce you to people on their networks. In addition, as Landy Chase, president of Rainmaker Associates, points out in *American Salesman*, by volunteering you may have the opportunity to get to know members of the Inner Circle. They could have powerful contacts.[7]

Be a reliable source of information. Before you tell the unemployed writer in the group that General Widget is hiring two writers, recheck that that is true. If your source is not reliable, then tell that to the writer. Inaccurate information builds false hopes and damages your own credibility.

Learn to work grapevines. Every group has a grapevine. You want to get plugged into it. The best way to do that is to be visible in the group. Once they see you are part of the group they will begin to share information. Be cool while you're waiting to be accepted. Don't ask too many questions. Share the information you do have.

Use your ten seconds well. In networking, says Lillian Bjorseth, a networking consultant in Chicago, people make their minds up about you in ten seconds. In those ten seconds they've made many decisions about you. Those decisions are about your moral character, success, economic heritage, social heritage, economic level, education, educational heritage, sophistication, and trustworthiness.[8]

In short, in ten seconds the group makes a response to your image. You want that image to highlight your strengths and mask your weaknesses.

Show Grace Under Pressure. Great leaders and great people are known for their grace under pressure. No matter what crisis they have at the office or at home, they don't conduct themselves a ways that will upset or annoy the group. That's the way you want to be, even if the boss is berating you or you just lost your $40,000 job. Loss of control and desperation are unwelcome in networks. And you will be perceived as desperate if you frantically go around the room and introduce yourself to massive numbers of people.

Things to Remember

- Networking is a multipurpose tool.
- Networking is about helping others who need help.
- Networking is a long-term activity.
- Have grace under pressure.

7

MAKING ALLIES
OF BABY BOOMERS

This chapter is must reading IF:

- You hate or fear Baby Boomers
- Baby Boomers hate or fear you
- Baby Boomers have the power in your office
- It seems you have nothing in common with Baby Boomers

Not long ago there was a cover story in *Fortune* entitled "Why Baby Busters Hate Baby Boomers."[1] The article emphasized that generational conflict is nothing new. In fact, conflict between generations is as old as the mother-in-law and daughter-in-law who can't get along. And did any of us, after the age of about fourteen, ever really get along with our parents?

SIX GENERATIONS

Right now in the United States, says Diane Crispell in *American Demographics*, there are *six* generations: the GI Generation, made up of those born before 1930; the Depression Generation, made up of people born between 1930 and 1939; the War Babies, born between 1940 and 1945; the Baby Boomers, born between 1946 and 1964; you, the Baby Bust Generation, born between 1965 and 1976; and the Baby

Boomlet Generation, made up of those born after 1977.[2] Depending on who's doing the counting, you can add or subtract a few years in most of these categories.

In subtle ways, or in blatantly obvious ways, each generation usually puts the knock on the generations that have come before or that come after. It reminds me the of old song in which parents wonder why kids can't be like they were—perfect in every way. But it *is* possible not only to get along but to be allies with those of another generation. In this chapter, I'll explain how you can make allies of the Baby Boomers.

MY RUN-INS

At work in the 1960s, I had my own private hell with the older generation. I was an eager beaver and therefore stood out. That made me a target for the elders to vent their spleen. I had to learn quickly how to handle it.

For example, there was a Pulitzer Prize winner associated with our public relations office. His day job was working on an East Coast newspaper. Seemingly out of nowhere, this award-winning writer came up to me one day and said, "You want to get ahead. Well, it won't be on my back." I was stunned, but I didn't scurry back to my desk and hide underneath it. If I had let him see my fear, this man would have tormented me forever. I told him I thought it was possible for us to have a good working relationship. I held out an olive branch that could help him save face. He went for it, and we worked together very well. Lessons learned: *Don't let them know that you're scared. And don't give up on the possibility of a friendship with another generation.*

There was also an incident when I was working on the Columbia University public relations account during the student riots in 1968. At the end of the riots, Grayson Kirk, Columbia's president, and David Truman, the chair of the trustees, came up to me and thanked me for what I had done. I was only twentysomething, and this was a big deal to me. What came next was an even bigger deal. They asked if they could have my telephone number in case they needed to reach me over the weekend. No one knew whether the riots would break out again.

The following Monday I was called in by my supervisor, Bob C. He was the "Boomer" in my life, the same type you're dealing with now. Bob C. cursed at me. He got all red in the face. He wagged his finger. He told me that I was trying to steal his day in the sun. As his rage ran its course, I realized two things. One, when I was asked for my telephone number I should also have given Bob's telephone number. Two, I didn't have to take this abuse from him. I thought about that and went up a level to see Bob C.'s boss. It worked. Bob C.'s boss spoke to Bob, and never again did he wag his finger at me. Lessons learned: *First of all, no matter how cautious you are, you're going to make mistakes dealing with the older generation. Second, you don't have to put up with bad behavior. Third, find an effective way to try to stop the abuse.*

BABY BOOMERS

I'm a member of the Silent Generation, those people who came of age in the conformist 1950s. But emotionally and in terms of my worldview, I could sometimes pass for a Baby Boomer. If you understand Baby Boomers, I think you'll find it easier to put up with them—and even enjoy them.

As Bruce Tulgan points out in *Managing Generation X*, "Boomers were raised to expect a high and steadily increasing standard of living." After World War II, much of the world was in a shambles, but the United States was experiencing record economic growth. Per capita income in the 1950s grew by 48 percent, and 60 percent of the population fit into the category called "middle class."[3]

If you were a young person in the 1950s, the United States was close to utopia. The family unit was still intact, and families were so child-centered they even took their vacations where the little ones could enjoy themselves. TV was new, and it had special programming for children such as the *Howdy Doody* show. Because of Boomers' sheer numbers— 79.4 million of them[4]—the world *had* to accommodate them. There were new playgrounds, new schools, new hospitals, all built just for them—and they knew it. The media made them celebrities. Whatever fad they were into made the cover of *Time*. In response to all this attention, Boomers began to assume they were special.

For Baby Boomers education was widely available, excellent in quality, and affordable back then. Baby Boomers thought nothing of going to graduate school after four long years of college. They were probably the most highly educated generation in American history.

Meanwhile, when many of them were in school—undergraduate or graduate—the cultural upheavals of the 1960s happened. Some Boomers embraced those movements with gusto. They campaigned against the Vietnam War, rigid sexual mores, and the values that their parents brought with them from the Great Depression. They got to feel very righteous about their own point of view. Plus, while they were trying to change the world, they also had a ball experimenting with different lifestyles and listening to a lot of music.

When it came time for them to finally enter the workforce, they once again wanted it all. And they were sure that they were going to get it all: easily available work that was also interesting; promotions; a loving, supportive family who didn't interfere with the job; the ability to grow on the job; and money— a lot of it. The Great American Job Machine was cranking out plenty of new positions; there were more than enough jobs to go around, even for the many young women who entered the workforce for the first time on a large scale. Both men and women went to large organizations like GM or GE and planned their strategies for climbing the ladder. Many of them made it to middle management. Some of them, such as Bill Clinton, made it to the top.

Along the way there were recessions, notably in 1974–75 and 1981–82. Some Boomers lost jobs. But they were able to get new ones, and often better ones, before too long. Their generation still had its magic—until downsizing came around in the late 1980s. This changed everything. Overnight the Boomers went from smug, well-paid executives to vulnerable working stiffs who could be out of a job at any time. Their graying hair made them especially vulnerable to layoffs. For the first time in their lives they felt gut-wrenching fear.

And it wasn't that easy anymore to get another job. There was simply less opportunity out there than when they were young. Harvard Business School professor Rosabeth Moss Kanter cites a study of managers who lost their jobs. For about 75 percent of them, there was economic hardship. Some laid-off Baby Boomers found they couldn't get another comparable job. Others found it took them a long time to find another job—or, at the new job, they had to take a pay cut.[5] In addition, downsizing brought about a flatter corporate organization; there was less upward mobility for the Boomers. Many had to face the fact that where they were was the best they'd ever do.

And those lucky enough to still have jobs keep looking over their shoulder for the ax. Meanwhile, some of them already had children in college. It was heartbreaking for them to see their grandiose expectations for the work world and their own financial destiny give way to an acceptance of the current realities of capitalism.

As a group, women among the Baby Boomers also had a dark night of the soul. They were finding how difficult it was to have it all. Also, despite their talent, drive, and sacrifices, they were bumping up against the glass ceiling.

In short, Boomers went from being the golden generation to being mere cogs in the capitalist system. Now employers expected them to be up to speed on technology. And as soon as they felt comfortable with DOS, the powers-that-be introduced Windows. Somehow the work world wasn't in the Boomers' control anymore.

This new adversity gives them a lot in common with you. As Generation X expert Karen Richie points out, so far your lives have been anything but golden. You've never known the Great American Job Machine. Many of you had to go through your parents' divorce. Many of you who lived with your mother faced poverty. Many of you had to take on a part-time job at a young age. By the time you were ready for college, inflation had made a college education a six-figure investment, on which you're probably still paying off loans. Now, downsizing has reduced the number and the quality of jobs open to you.[6]

What's obvious to me is that there's now plenty of common ground between you and the Baby Boomers—if you can both forget the resentments you have against each other. Those resentments are par for the course when two generations look at each other. I remember that plenty of Baby Boomers had resentments over the success of the Silent Generation. Boomers thought it had been easier for the Silents to get ahead, since there had been fewer of them. Boomers thought it was easier for the Silents to get into Ivy League colleges because, again, there were fewer of them. And Boomers resented the fact that these people—who were not brighter or more able—were the bosses.

The Boomers and your generation have had your beefs about each other. According to *Fortune*'s Suneel Ratan, you feel that the Baby Boomers got the best of everything, from free (and disease-free) love to the good jobs in the workplace. Boomers say you're arrogant and aren't willing to pay your dues.[7] Now, even if all that were true—and it probably isn't—this kind of mindset isn't going to help you make allies of the Boomers. Boomers were reared to expect a lot of themselves and the world. Often neither, from their point of view, measured up.

At this point in your career, it's in your professional self-interest to make friends with the Baby Boomers. At this point in *their* careers, Baby Boomers still have tremendous power in the workplace. They know a lot of people—useful connections for you. They also know how the system works, and they could be excellent mentors for you. According to Wayne Johnson, Baby Boomers are not likely to retire soon. Because they didn't sock enough away for retirement, they'll probably keep working even after they hit sixty-five.[8] So they will be a force to contend with for a while.

COMPASSION

One way to get through the barriers separating you from the Baby Boomers is old-fashioned compassion. Did you ever lose anything that was important to you? Remember how you felt? Well, that's how the Baby Boomers feel. They've lost their belief that the world can be made perfect. They've lost their ability to control the workplace. And they've lost their dream of never doing anything just because they *had* to do it. Now they're going to work every day—because they have to.

Also, Baby Boomers are afraid of getting old and out of touch. If you feel for them, steer them to what's new. Discuss an article you read in *Wired* and ask them if they want to borrow your copy. Treat them to lunch and let them know how young people think. They may want to go and hear a band with you. Think to invite them.

COMMON GROUND

How else can you become allies with Baby Boomers? As I mentioned earlier, a good strategy is finding common ground. What do you two have in common? Plenty, now.

Both you and the Baby Boomers are disillusioned with the work world. (Indeed, who isn't?) Both of you had certain expectations about the work world. You anticipated that your job would be fulfilling, be meaningful, and make a difference. But at this point in the evolution of capitalism, most of the work that could be perceived as meaningful—in education or medicine, for example—often doesn't pay enough to make ends meet. More and more people are coming to view work not as a means of self-fulfillment but as a way to put bread on the table.

As management consultant Michael Hammer points out, this way of seeing work—as economic survival—is a relatively recent development in the history of capitalism. Before this viewpoint became dominant, many looked upon their work as their calling or vocation. The economic aspects were acknowledged but not dwelled on.[9] You and Baby Boomers have a lot to discuss about the new realities of the workplace.

Both you and the Baby Boomers probably have been affected by divorce, only in different ways. You've known what it is to have your parents splitting up and the financial ramifications of that. Baby Boomers are the ones getting divorces nowdays and feeling how that translates into alimony, child support, and joint custody. How do you think marriage will fare in the twenty-first century? That's something the two of you can discuss.

You're both highly dependent on technology. Instead of complaining how inept Baby Boomers are with technology, which many of you do, why not help them become as adept as you are? The catch: You have to see to it that they're willing to accept your help. Explain how you came across something really interesting on the World Wide Web. Would they like to see it? If so, ask them what else they'd like to see on the Web, and show them how to get there.

Both Boomers and you are highly visual. At meetings and in reports you know how to discuss things in visual terms. That's how both your generations think—only you more so. That sets you both against the Silents, a pre-TV generation.

You're both likely to be cynical. Aging, getting fat, the probable necessity of working past sixty-five, trying to send their children to the college of their choice—all this has turned many formerly idealistic Baby Boomers into cynics. As a generation you're known for your cynicism. That makes for a good match. I'm sure you can share a lot of insider jokes about the workplace.

And being allies doesn't mean you have to have a love-in. It does mean that you're mutually useful to one another. Baby Boomers are too massive a force in the workplace for you not to use. They're as important a resource as your college degree or your PC.

Things to Remember

- Generational strife has always existed.
- If you learn who the Baby Boomers really are, you'll enjoy them.
- Baby Boomers are going through a rough time. Be compassionate and think about ways you can help them out. That will help make them your allies.
- Your generations aren't so far apart anymore. You can leverage what you now have in common to become allies.

8

IMAGE

This chapter is must reading IF:

- You are in a crisis
- Somebody has damaged your image
- You feel you need an image fix
- You don't know what your image is

Whether you like it or not, agree with it or not, think it's unfair or not, people judge you by your image.

At one time, Michael Jackson's image was that of a brilliant performer. Then a cloud settled over that image. Jackson's popularity and record sales have been affected.

Political strategist Dick Morris had an excellent professional reputation. Then the tabloid *Star* published an exposé of what Morris allegedly did in his off-duty hours. Now people are speculating that his image may never recover.

All the good Lee Iacocca accomplished at Chrysler was quickly forgotten when he joined forces with Kirk Kerkorian and his image became that of a corporate raider.

Every young person starting out in a job has an image. If you're not satisfied with that image, or you've outgrown it, you can change it.

NO IMAGE = IMPOSSIBILITY

There is no such thing as not having an image. If you think you don't have an image, then what people are probably saying about you is this: You're neither here nor there; you're wishy-washy; and you don't pay enough attention to making a statement about yourself. I knew a man who had a Ph.D. in philosophy. He was a near genius. But he didn't take pains with his image. Around the office his nickname was "the Unmade Bed." For all his intelligence and drive, he didn't get anywhere. In fact, he was let go in the first wave of layoffs.

If you don't work on your image, that image will be formed primarily by the impressions of people who work with you. That's giving a lot of power to people who might not have your best interests uppermost in their minds. Not cultivating an image puts you on the defensive, instead of where you should be—on the offensive. The Republican Party has an image. The Democratic Party has an image. ValueJet has an image. Bill Clinton has an image. The mailboy has an image. And if those people haven't given a lot of thought to that image, they're not very savvy.

Image starts early. A speech I delivered in 1972 is now on the Internet. My image was starting to develop way back then—and I just didn't realize it.

WHAT IS IMAGE?

Your image is the bundle of signals you give off. Your image includes just about everything: your clothes, your manners, the music you listen to, the kind of writing paper you use, the movies you see, the language you use, the suggestions you make at meetings.

Your image works effectively only if it's integrated. For example, suppose you wear conservative suits and are meticulous in your work but are overly gregarious in your personal manner. That discontinuity would confuse people. In managing your image you don't want your appearance to say one thing and your behavior to say another.

Also, there shouldn't be major incongruities between what your image is inside the office and what your image is in the community.

That will also confuse people. They may even think that you are unstable.

You might say that your image is a shorthand way of telling the world what you're about. Jay Leno's image says: "I'm a nice guy—and also pretty funny." Bill Clinton's image says: "Like me." Actress Patty Duke's image says: "I've been through the wringer."

What is your image saying? Maybe you should ask a friend about this.

And, as Roger Ailes, media adviser to U.S. presidents and to corporate CEOs, always stresses: Folks make up their mind about your image almost instantly.[1]

I can't tell you the number of times I've gone into CEOs' offices knowing I have a very brief time to make my pitch—and my impression. Those CEOs don't see "Bob Dilenschneider, good citizen and entrepreneur." Rather, as I'm sitting there making my pitch, they see "management consultant who can or cannot help me." If the CEOs decide that I can't help them, they make that decision fast— and have been known to bid me "good day" and walk out of the room! Somehow, my image didn't communicate "can be of use to you." As a result, there's nothing I can do to pry loose that piece of business. It's primarily my image that gets, or doesn't get, new business. For- tunately, most times my image communicates to clients: "Yes, I'm the one to help you."

IT'S A BIG WORLD OUT THERE

Image is often different around the world. In the Northeast, people tend to be aggressive but formal. In the Pacific Northwest, people tend to be laid back and more casual. And you have to know things like that before you go there and present yourself. Years ago in California there was tremendous criticism about the "pushy" New Yorkers who had moved there. By now native-born Californians have adjusted to the New York image. But I still have to tone down my drive and slow down my pace when I go Los Angeles or San Francisco from New York.

One hard-charging woman went to a utility company in L.A. for a job interview. Nothing in her resumé indicated she was born and raised in Brooklyn, but the interviewer, who hates New Yorkers, cut the interview short and didn't even have her meet his boss. The woman hadn't done her homework. She could have called the L.A. Chamber of Commerce or the local branch of her professional organization. She should have found out what kind of image those in California have of folks from the New York area.

Overseas, the challenge is the same. If you're going to do business in China, you have to have a different image than you would have in Japan. In Italy, I'm relaxed. In France, I'm more formal.

IMAGES IN PROFESSIONS

In law school or medical school, you not only learn a profession, you become socialized in how to act appropriately in those professions. In your first few months at GE or McKinsey Consulting, you will also be socialized to conform to those organizations' images. In the seminary, a young man training to be a Roman Catholic priest learns how to comport himself in a priestly manner.

If you enter a profession and don't bother to adapt to the overall image in the field, or resist adapting to it, you're going to be in trouble. Some mavericks, like Campbell's chairman-CEO-president David Johnson, have managed to get away with it. But they're usually outstanding at what they do.

As a public relations strategist, I am expected to be gregarious and sure of myself. If I were introverted and insecure, people would be puzzled at first, then angry that I had violated their expectations. Haven't you ever been angry that a medical doctor didn't "act like a doctor should"?

Professional image brings with it a set of expectations. You have to be willing—and able—to conform to those expectations.

CHANGING TIMES

Your image will probably change with the times. It might also change if you switch jobs or if your organization adopts a new type of organizational culture. In a small trade association your image might be like that of the absent-minded professor. In a large consumer products company your image might be staid and highly professional. But if a new CEO comes in and is a change agent, you may have to become more energetic and put in more "face time." Part of Madonna's marketing genius is that she can sense when it's time to change her image.

When I first started out in business, the prevailing image for an ambitious man was an energetic persona. You had to be careful not to become too energetic, though, because that could lead people to think you were not entirely focused and in control. For a woman, once she was married, the prevailing image at that time was to be a partner to her husband. She could have other interests such as art or charity work or even a job—but her "core competency" was helping Mr. Man.

How that has changed! Energetic is no longer enough. An ambitious man must now have more to him than just a high energy level. In addition to earning a living I'm now expected to be sensitive, concerned about the world, and helpful to others. And although women might still be seen in terms of partnership with their significant other, more is expected of them, too. Women are expected to help themselves—and also exhibit a lot of other qualities. If Marilyn Monroe returned today her "sex-goddess" persona would not be enough. She would probably be expected to fund-raise for AIDS.

This gender issue is far from being solved, both for men and for women. How sensitive ought I be? If my client loses a job, should we both sit down and shed a few tears? Must a woman, to be perceived as "feminine," still bring in home-baked cookies? My best take on it is that both sexes should avoid playing into stereotypes. On Monday I shouldn't spend the day saying how I can't wait until *Monday Night Football,* and women shouldn't feel that they *must* talk about their children. Neither should show favoritism to any gender. What counts is performance. I've rarely seen a manager fail who's consistently rewarded performance.

OUT OF THE CLOSET

At one time in society we didn't talk openly about image. That seemed too manipulative. You were expected to pick up the right way to present yourself from the members of your family. That's primarily why people from professional families were so successful back then. They knew the rules. They knew how to present themselves. They knew enough not to discuss business at the Christmas party.

Back then, if your bosses were doing your annual review and noticed something they didn't like in your image, they might recommend that you be more "businesslike." But you had to figure out what they meant.

Again, things have changed since then! In *Hispanic* magazine, Kim and Edward Valdez come right out and tell their readers they "must project the image your company expects of its employees and that your manager desires in his or her subordinates."[2] (Note that the authors aren't telling Hispanic readers to just be themselves, or to celebrate their ethnic heritage.) Now there is actually an Institute for Image Management in San Francisco. Companies refer executives to the institute to learn how to enhance their image.

BENEFITS OF A GOOD IMAGE

With image, the stakes are high. That's because image is everything. Image is the foundation of success—both for big companies like Colgate-Palmolive, and for individuals like you. I work with many organizations that want "just the right image." When they get it, it directly affects their bottom line. In *Reputation*, Charles Fombrun points out that a good image allows organizations to:

- Charge premium prices for their products
- Achieve stability in revenues
- Pay lower prices for purchases
- Attract top people to work at the organization
- Obtain greater loyalty from employees and customers
- Receive greater latitude to act by constituents
- Encounter fewer crises[3]

For you, as an individual, the benefits of a good image can also be profound. I've seen young people with good images enjoy:

- **The halo effect.** Everything you do is viewed with an expectation that it will be excellent.

- **Increased latitude to act.** The powers-that-be don't keep you on a short leash.

- **More money.** For example, Susan Bixler in *The Professional Image* cites a study by Judith Walters of Fairleigh Dickinson University. The study was focused on professional appearance. "Before" (that is, not highly professional-looking) and "after" (that is, highly professional-looking) photos with identical resumés were sent to more than a one thousand companies. Recipients were asked to determine a starting salary for the person in the photo. Those who had the "after" pictures assigned salaries 8 to 20 percent higher than the salaries assigned to the "before."[4]

- **Greater cooperation from all constituencies.** People like working with you.

- **Self-assurance.** You recognize that you have a good image in place, and you're not insecurely monitoring yourself all the time.

- **Access to resources.** People help you get what you need to get the job done.

- **Nonproblematic relationships with "difficult" people.** Your image is oriented not to push any of the usual hot buttons.

- **Broader career options.** The right image can help people see you in a number of roles. If you are a writer, for instance, they can also see you in a leadership role.

CREATING YOUR IMAGE

The image you create for yourself depends on what you want. Maybe what you want is for the powers-that-be to perceive you as promotable. Maybe you want just to be left alone to do your work. Or perhaps you want to be seen as a leader. What you want is how you should *appear*. That's the bottom line.

But your image must have substance. The days of an empty suit—or an empty skirt—are over. Image alone is not enough. Back in the 1950s and 1960s, many people could get away with just looking the part. There were vice presidents who looked just like vice presidents, and they could do well for themselves even if they weren't great leaders or had no special expertise. But today you're expected to present yourself well *and* have something unique to offer the marketplace. Both are essential. On the other hand, if you have plenty of substance but you don't have a suitable image, you probably won't go too far.

Image basically comes down to certain habits you acquire. Let's say Pete has always had good grooming habits, and his image has always been that of a man who takes good care of himself. Another part of his image is his impeccable manners. In an age of barbarian behavior, Pete stands out because he has a habit of treating everyone with respect. Before he enters your office, he asks if it's a good time to see you; after he completes a transaction with you, he'll make sincere inquiries about your family. People like to have Pete around. Another of Pete's habits is that he sees the positive aspects of a problem. As a result, bosses can always count on him to raise the morale at a meeting.

What Pete does is cultivate an image—a good image. That's what image is. What image *isn't* is a persona of the day or a flavor of the month. It doesn't work out if today in the office you'll "act" like a team player, tomorrow you "act" like a creative genius who only works alone, and the next day you "act" like a leader. You can't put on an "act" anymore. You have to develop a series of behaviors that continually give off the right signals.

For example, suppose you want to be perceived as promotable. Every day you should:

Dress like the level above you. Don't just dress well when you have an official meeting with the boss. People see you every day. And it isn't simply your boss who decides whether you get promoted. Usually a number of other people also have input.

Be helpful. Those who get promoted are seen to be genuinely interested in others' well-being. That's because the higher you go in a company, the more interaction you'll have. Few companies want a narcissist.

Establish friendly relationships in other departments. Those connections will help you get a promotion and be useful to you after you are promoted.

Be energetic. People who get ahead always have an extra tank of energy to switch over to. But you don't want to seem *too* animated.

Be relaxed. Given the stress and downsizing in the job market, nobody wants a Chicken Little around screaming, "The sky is falling, the sky is falling." A relaxed persona will give your superiors confidence in you.

Go the extra mile—whatever that mile is. Maybe the boss, or the boss's boss, needs a report right away. Volunteer to do it. You want to get a reputation for being dependable and productive during crises.

Have a sense of humor. That shows you can detach yourself from a situation and look at things objectively. You want your habits of humor to be low-key, however. A belly laugh is seldom appropriate in the workplace, unless the boss leads the merriment. Smile instead.

Be eager to learn. Go for a degree if the organization encourages that. Often just being in an MBA program gives you status and makes people see you as a go-getter. On the other hand, if the organization is very frenetic, it might not look kindly on your spending time getting a degree for yourself.

Be enthusiastic. Companies *say* they want to hear your reservations about a project, but they often really don't. They might label you as negative. The workplace is not a democracy where there is freedom of speech.

These are just some of the habits you need to acquire if you want to get ahead. You will acquire them slowly, through trial and error. For example, if you want to be perceived as energetic, it might take time to get the rhythm right. At first you might come across simply as hyperanimated. Then you will realize that, just like an athlete, you have to pace yourself. You want to be perceived as being just as energetic at 7 P.M. as you are at 9 A.M., which means *not* enjoying a good, long yawn and *not* confiding in people how you can't wait to get home and go to sleep. Often the powers-that-be judge your energy level by how you handle yourself *after* official quitting time.

SYMBOLISM

The heartbeat of image is symbolism. That's because people see the world symbolically. I don't see Joe as Joe; I see Joe as a good worker. Image reduces people to manageable concepts so that we can deal with them. Image is a fairly easy way to communicate to the world who you are—and the good news is, you can plan for it ahead of time.

Since I want to appear at the top of my game, I don't take copious notes during a meeting. If there's no one to take notes, I discreetly run a tape recorder. Why? Because if the clients see me as a compulsive note taker, I'm going to lose points in their eyes. I won't look like an executive.

What do you want to be "seen as"? When you're thinking about your image, think what every aspect of your behavior symbolizes— because that's how your colleagues and superiors judge you. For example:

- You come in late frequently. Do people see that as disinterest in your work? When you're the last to leave the office at night, do people see this as being a good soldier, or as being too inefficient in getting your work done on time?

- You eat lunch with the bosses. Do your colleagues see this as a threat, or just as smart business? If they see it as a threat, should you come up with a symbolic gesture—like bringing in dough-nuts on Friday—to demonstrate that you're still one of the gang?

- You're going for an MBA at night. Do your superiors see that as a waste of time, or as a big help to the organization?

- The vice president publicly thanked you at the meeting. How do people see your ability to take praise?

- How does the organization where you're interviewing see your willingness to leave your current job after eighteen months? Should you wait longer?

- You took off the day your dog died. How did people at work see that? Would it have been better for your image if you had just called in sick rather than revealing the real reason to coworkers?

- You wear expensive clothes. Do people see that as putting them down?

THE TIME COMES

With so much change going on in your life and in the world of business, it's inevitable that you might also need to modify, or even overhaul, your image. How do you know when it's time? Here are some guideposts:

- You don't think your image is helping you to achieve the next success you want. It helped you in the past, but it isn't helping with your present objectives.

- Someone has told you that you're being self-defeating in how you handle yourself.
- Your image no longer represents you. It's giving off misleading signals.
- You wish you had the courage to make changes in your image.
- You're in a crisis.

Changing an image can be difficult. We're not sure we can pull it off, and we don't know what reception our new persona will get in the office. But sometimes, such as in a crisis, it's necessary. Bart L. sensed that his laid-*back* image contributed to his getting laid *off*. So he sees Job Number One as creating a more energetic, responsive image.

The best approach in image change is to take it slowly and consider the image "reconfiguration" as a type of experiment—an experiment that may or may not work. Build up new habits at a pace you can handle. That pace should be gradual enough so you can make corrections in what you're trying to do without people being too aware of it.

Even with the right pacing, at some point people are going to notice your emerging new image, and they may comment. You have to be prepared to give them a logical explanation of why you're doing what you're doing. I wouldn't advise mentioning the word "image." That opens a whole can of worms. They might ask, "What was wrong with your old image?" "Why do you need a new image, are you shooting for a promotion?" "Do you really think changing your image will help?" "What's so important about an image?"

There are myriad ways to explain why you're becoming different. You can say that you picked up some tips in a seminar. That your spouse made these suggestions. That your mentor shared some recommendations with you. Or you can can use your sense of humor to deflect their interest. For example, you can make light of your power tie. In short, there are countless ways you can satisfy the curiosity of coworkers and subordinates without violating your own sense of privacy.

As you try out aspects of a new image and sense they're not

working well, don't stay with them. Recreating an image is a tough job. You will probably make mistakes. Approach this the way an editor of a film would—that is, most of what you try will likely wind up on the cutting room floor. Just sweep up the mess and keep working.

Things to Remember

- Everyone has an image, and that image should change with the times.
- The right image brings profound benefits.
- Image is a series of habits you integrate.
- Image and image change require trial and error.

9

HAVING INFLUENCE
AT ANY LEVEL

This chapter is must reading IF:

- You believe in talent
- You feel powerless at work
- You're not able to sell your ideas
- Your job is threatened

If someone said you were influential, would you be flattered or offended? Probably a little of both.

THE GENERATIONS AND INFLUENCE

In my generation we'd be quite flattered. "Influential" signified a lot of positive things to us, ranging from knowing how to get things done to relating well to people.

But for your generation "influential" brings up images of your parents' generation. It seems to belong to another era. And "influential" suggests manipulation. It's true, some people in positions of influence *do* manipulate. Usually, though, they're not very successful. True influence requires substance. You have to be able to offer something of substance in exchange for the other person's cooperation, ideas, or whatever.

Another thing your generation tends to say about influence is that you don't want to get entangled in the web of obligations that influence involves. Instead, you say, you'll get what you want purely on talent. After all, isn't this new economy a meritocracy? Shouldn't your talent win out? Well, from my experience, I've never seen talent alone win the day. There always has to be a sponsor or champion involved to get people to notice someone's talent. That help is frequently called the "big break." And you make the big break happen by connecting with a broad range of people—in other words, by creating a sphere of influence.

In this chapter I'll discuss how you can increase your influence at work, even if you have an entry level position. All of us have more influence than we think. There's no correlation between your rank in an organization and your degree of influence. Secretaries are often the most influential people in a company. An assistant manager I knew at an insurance company practically ran the department.

DEFINING INFLUENCE

What *is* "influence"? One of the best definitions I've come across was in a *Time* magazine cover story, *"The 25 Most Influential People in America."* According to *Time,* "Being influential is the reward of successful salesmanship, the validation of personal passion, the visible sign of individual merit."[1]

INFLUENCE AND POWER

Influence is different from power. Power, as we've come to know it, is usually the power of position. Your bosses have power by virtue of the fact that they're the bosses; if a boss is demoted, that power disappears immediately. Also, the minute a chief executive officer is no longer CEO, the power vanishes. There are exceptions; Edwin Artzt, former CEO of Procter & Gamble, became CEO of an Italian company after retiring. Another former Procter & Gamble CEO, John Smale, was able to work for three years supervising General Motors. But in general, power ends when the CEO job ends.

Anyone's power—even the CEO's power—can be taken away. The organization can fire you. It can demote you. But your *influence* is *yours.* You're the only one who can take away your influence at work.

You do that by compromising your credibility. I've seen many people screw up by overpromising—and then underdelivering.

Some people can have both power and influence. Former president Ronald Reagan was such a person. During Camelot, the Kennedys had both. According to *Time*, though, President Clinton is a man of power—but not influence.[2] In most organizations, it's not enough to have power. To get things done, the powerful people also need influence. That's why there's so much "politicking" in the workplace. That's how things get done.

Probably the person who was most brilliant in the art of influence throughout history was Jesus Christ. Though he had no worldly riches, he was able to persuade twelve men to leave their way of life and follow him. He used a variety of instruments, ranging from eloquent speaking to miracles, to persuade the public to embrace his point of view. His death, which his disciples described in ritualistic fashion, had profound influence. Rituals are important to influence.

THE MINDSET FOR INFLUENCE

A WORLD OF ALLIES

Being influential starts with a mindset. In *Influence Without Authority*, Allan Cohen and David Bradford point out that influence begins with a thinking pattern—specifically, with the belief that all those people at your workplace are potential allies. And Cohen and Bradford mean *all*. They suggest that you even make your boss an ally or strategic partner.[3] I agree.

This mindset is very different from how we usually see the world. Because we are a competitive society, we tend to see the workplace as consisting of those we can run rings around and those who are clearly superior to us. We also tend to divide the workplace into friends and nonfriends. We wouldn't hesitate to call upon a friend for help, but we're standoffish with the nonfriends. Then there is a group in work whom we would call our allies. We know we can count on them for resources. But usually this isn't a large group.

This way of thinking eliminates a lot of people from being allies. However, it is possible to have just about every person in your workplace as a potential ally. All it takes is a certain point of view.

And that point of view is: *This person could be an ally down the road. I had better get to know that individual and what he or she is all about.* Your key ally could work in the mailroom or in the CEO's office. Resources come in all kinds of packages.

This ally, or partner, mindset is the heartbeat of influence. In "Negotiating to Shift Power Without Losing Influence," Leonard Marcus points out that influence comes from "new ways to frame and conduct the business of your institution."[4] Walk into a meeting, and the traditional way of framing would be to divide the attendees into competitors, noncompetitors, friends, people we don't like, boss's friends, snitches, idiots, and flaming idiots. For you to reframe that collection of people as a roomful of potential allies is pretty radical, but it's the prerequisite of influence. Influential people in your organization have been doing it for years. They don't think, "Is this person nice?" They think, "Is this person a useful resource to me?"

START PLAYING

Another change you might have to make is your willingness to participate in the dynamics of workplace influence. In a workshop a friend of mine attended, influence expert Jeffrey Pfeffer emphasized the importance of being in the game. "A lot of people at large companies," explains Pfeffer, "have the 'passover' rule." They think that if they keep their head down and blend in, nothing bad will happen to them.[5]

Before there was a global economy, before downsizing, it was possible to sit out the game. No more. The global economy has made jobs precarious. Now you have to have influence to protect your job. That's what "air cover" is all about. "Air cover" means that those in higher positions will protect you. Those who survive a layoff are usually those who are being protected; they got that protection through influence. Also, in a downsized world you're more visible and have more responsibility; to deal with that you need influence. You can't go to work any more and assume you'll be okay if you just do your work. In fact, you can't do many of today's new jobs at all without knowing how to tap into all sorts of resources. And that means being influential. "Influencing" has been written into your job description.

YOUR VALUES

The third piece in the new mindset you must develop is to come to terms with your values. Influencing is not a value-free activity. We all have codes of conduct for how we'll influence. What's yours? What are you willing to do while influencing, and what will you not do? For example, Jeffrey Pfeffer points out in his book *Managing With Power* that "flattery or ingratiation is a very effective technique of interpersonal influence."[6] But maybe you're against the idea of flattering anyone. Well, those are your values, and you shouldn't go against them. There are many other ways in which you can exert influence. There's no one influence strategy or technique you must embrace.

INFLUENCE STRATEGIES

How do you influence? There are workshops, courses, and books on this. But the simplest explanation of influence strategies is probably Robert Cialdini's *Influence: The Psychology of Persuasion*. As the title says, influence is really getting someone else to agree with our point of view. In ancient Greece they wrote books and plays to win over people to a certain point of view; today you express your point of view on TV and the Internet. But it's all the same. You want people to agree with you and take the action you recommend. To be effective, teachers, ministers, agents, and many other professionals must be influential.

In *Influence*, Cialdini introduces six principles, or weapons, of influence:

- **Reciprocation,** or the old give and take
- **Commitment and consistency,** or the human tendency to file new information in familiar grooves (or boxes) in the mind
- **Social proof,** or the power of what everybody is thinking (or seems to be thinking)
- **Liking,** or the tendency to deal with people you're attracted to
- **Authority,** or the deference we pay to the experts
- **Scarcity,** or the idea that potentially losing something makes the commodity more valuable[7]

Let's look at those six and see how you can participate in the influence game.

RECIPROCITY

In my book *Power and Influence*, I call this the "favor bank."[8] I like the image of a bank because in reciprocity, just as in a bank, we're continually putting in and withdrawing favors. And as with a bank, if there are more withdrawals than deposits, you'd better find some fresh funds to deposit.

Reciprocity is perhaps the simplest strategy in influence. Just think back to those who've done favors for you at work. Maybe a coworker followed you to the car dealer to have your car serviced, took you back to work, and again drove you to the dealer. That's a big favor. How did you repay it? Or are you still repaying it? There is something hard-wired in human nature that makes us reciprocate. Instinctively, we seem to know there is no free lunch.

In the favor bank you build up obligations or debts. Some debts you owe. Other debts people owe you. That sense of obligation underlies many transactions in the workplace. If Joe the accountant owes you a favor for helping his daughter get a job, then you can feel perfectly comfortable going to Joe and getting insider information about the reorganization.

In his book, Cialdini discusses the power of reciprocity. He cites research showing that even a small favor—like bringing in a Coke for another person—imposes an obligation. The person who received the Coke feels compelled to reciprocate somehow. By giving out a free flower, the Hare Krishna imposed an obligation, and the person who received the flower—the Krishna refused to take it back—felt compelled to make a donation.[9]

Every day at work, people have been imposing obligations on you, although you might not have realized it. You ask the boss on short notice for this Monday off, and she says yes. That's an obligation. So if she wants you to stay late one Friday night, you'll most likely comply. You owe her.

Since all the people you work with are potential allies, it will seem natural that you help them out. After all, you're on the same side. You share common ground. But make sure you get paid back. I know of one naïve woman who did a lot of favors and wasn't concerned about people paying her back. Her coworkers saw her as a loose cannon because she wasn't playing the reciprocity game according to the rules. The rules are clear: You play, you pay.

Many young people ask me: Is it ever possible to have the brass in debt to you? The answer is yes. You can have "accounts receivable" from top people in the organization. They need to get things done just like everyone else. An executive I knew was going through a rough time and couldn't concentrate on the speech he was working on with his speechwriter. The speechwriter took over a great deal of responsibility for preparing the speech, and the executive knew he was in debt for that. If you have accounts receivable on the executive wing, don't be shy about collecting. Executives got where they are because they understand this bartering system in an organization.

COMMITMENT AND CONSISTENCY

We all tend to stay in a certain pattern. Maybe it's buying exotic fish for our tank. It would be difficult to change this pattern and, say, buy white mice or birds. This influence strategy is based on our human craving for sameness. Sameness makes everything, including decision making, easier. When you give to charity, is it the same charity, such as for cancer or MS, or do you switch every year? I bet you rarely switch.

If you want to sell an idea or proposal to your coworkers, put it in the form of something they already know. For example, reengineering could have been introduced into the organization by comparing it and contrasting it to Total Quality Management, a concept that is already known to people. That helps ground the audience.

The smart boss who wants you to take courses approaches you with what you already know: that the company has a tradition of intellectual excellence. Given that tradition, it seems to be a logical extension that you would be enthusiastic about taking one or two courses in your field. The boss can push the advisability of taking the second course once you're in the first course. The boss builds on the commitment.

Most people don't like new ideas. That's why good speakers will talk in terms of an analogy, or what's already familiar to the audience. If they want to discuss cyberspace, they discuss it in terms of an analogy such as the printing press. If you're trying to sell your coworkers on joining a white-collar union, speak in terms of a union they understand such as the AFL-CIO. Then, toward the end of your pitch, point out how your union will differ—in positive ways—from the AFL-CIO.

SOCIAL PROOF

What *everybody else* is doing influences what *we do*. Children know that. They let you know that all the fourth grade at St. Aloysius has been to the Baseball Hall of Fame. Given that, how can you resist taking *your* child? Pfeffer demonstrates this power of social proof when he refers to the infamous 1964 Kitty Genovese murder case in New York. Despite her ongoing loud screams as she was being killed, no neighbors came to Genovese's aid. Pfeffer explains this phenomenon in terms of social proof. No one was helping, therefore no one went to help. The old herd instinct.[10]

If you want the boss to buy a certain type of software, cite all the other companies that are using it. If your subordinates don't like the summer schedule of working longer hours Monday through Thursday and a half day on Friday, mention the other organizations using this system. Point out that it's been in force at headquarters for two years and that most of the workforce has indicated in a survey how much they like the summer hours.

What's important is that you select your social proof from groups your coworkers or superiors respect. If you're GE and you tell your subordinates a small company in Akron, Ohio, is already doing what they will be doing, it won't work. In an auto company several years ago, a subordinate was resisting learning how to use a computer. The boss took her out to lunch and explained how everyone else in the department was already on board in terms of computers. Obviously, she was odd person out. That afternoon, she started to learn how to operate the computer. If you want to sell your daughter's Girl Scout cookies at work, tell your prospects everyone else is buying, and cite names of people or departments.

LIKING

When the academic market collapsed in the 1970s, mentors told graduate students looking for work not to worry about keeping a job. Rather, they advised, just get a job and then make sure "they like you." Even those in the highly cerebral corridors of academia recognized the power of being liked.

Yes, we live in a high-tech world, but that very old-fashioned quality of being liked still has tremendous clout. People hire and promote those they like. One manager, after firing a writer, said to me, "I never liked her." That's how he summed up the whole relationship.

Cialdini points out that "we like people who are similar to us."[11] This brings you back to organizational culture. Go only where you fit in. If you don't fit in, you're not going to be able to influence. You'll be ignored. Or tormented.

If you think you need to become more likeable, take a sincere interest in other people. That means what's happening in their world becomes as important to you as what's happening in yours. There's no way of feigning this interest; if you try, your body language will give you away. Your sense of caring, says Daniel Goleman in *Emotional Intelligence*, must be real. And, if it's real, it will register in our body language. Goleman points out that 90 percent of communication of emotion is nonverbal.[12] Many people in the office go through the motions of caring about you, but they're usually only busybodies— and everybody knows that.

AUTHORITY

I knew a clever woman with a baby boy and a difficult mother-in-law. The mother-in-law kept insisting that the baby was too old to be sucking his thumb. That wasn't true, but the woman reported to her mother-in-law that she had consulted a child therapist, who thought thumb-sucking at two years of age was okay. The woman got the results she wanted by citing an authority. The mother-in-law backed off.

Appealing to authority is a fundamental element of persuasion. You learn it in the first few days of Freshman Composition. You also learn that not all sources of authority are equal. If you want your coworkers to come around to your way of thinking about the company's future, it wouldn't be all that persuasive to cite the annual report or the organization's newsletter. What *would* get them to sit up and listen is for you to quote a few security analysts.

But this strategy has to be used with caution. If you *only* appeal to outside authority, you could come across as not having the self-assurance to have an opinion of your own. I vividly remember how in grad school one eager beaver cited all sorts of authorities in a paper. The professor wrote, "But what do *you* think?"

SCARCITY

This is a strategy movie stars know well. So as not to be overexposed, and therefore less valuable, movie stars will limit the number of pictures they do. More isn't always better.

To become a prime influencer in your organization, move toward controlling the scarce resources in the organization. Let's say that the scarce resource is knowledge, and you and your team are an in-house think tank with a reputation for providing on-target information. That gives you tremendous influence. Everyone wants access to you, wants you to work on their projects, and wants you to present the information to customers.

Other scarce resources include time off, the fleet of company cars, capital for product development, access to the executive wing, and innovation the company will support. Whoever controls these has clout. Smart senators try to navigate to committee chairmanships that administer scarce resources, such as money.

You can even create your own scarcity. Your time, for example. If you're not always hanging around your office, it's going to be more difficult for people to gain access to you. Being busy is a surefire strategy in influencing. Those in demand are those not easily available. One of the great coups in influencing is for someone to have to leave a meeting early in order to get to another meeting.

But you don't want to become *too* scarce. Suppose your boss allowed you to work at home four days a week. Would that be a good idea politically? In some offices the more "face time" you put in, the more secure your position.

Things to Remember

- In the new economy, influence is a have-to.
- Influence doesn't mean manipulation.
- The world is full of allies.
- Sitting out the game is not an option.
- The key strategies are reciprocity, commitment and consistency, social proof, liking, authority, and scarcity.

10

SCHOOL

This chapter is must reading IF

- You're wondering whether going to school is worth the time and money
- You're thinking about leaving or returning to school
- You sense that you need more training in your field

School—and plenty of it. That's one thing you, the Baby Boomers and even my generation have in common.

INTELLECTUAL CAPITAL

After high school, it was college. After college, it might have been graduate school or professional school for an MA in math or a degree in medicine. Now, since we're in the Information Age, school is something you constantly think about. You struggle to decide: Should you go back to the university part-time for a certificate in finance or a few courses in mass media? Or maybe you should invest in going back full-time. In that way you might be able to start a new career in business or film, or significantly enhance the career you have now.

You probably know some people who changed their lives by returning to school. Perhaps they were drifting in their jobs. Then Eileen went back to school to get certified in teaching. As a high school teacher of business she's happy—and gets the summers off. John might have gone back to school for a graduate degree in social work, and today he's teaching social work in a top school and organizing tenant groups in the community. He loves the variety. Perhaps after college Jennifer discovered she was talented in computers, so she left a job she hated in advertising and went back to school for a degree in information management.

Higher education is the engine of the information economy. It helps supply the intellectual capital that "finances" the new economy. Almost daily I'm suggesting a course, seminar, or degree program to someone. I try to find the time to take courses myself.

ASSESSING THE INVESTMENT

Investing in higher education, like investing in a mutual fund, is a serious decision. Before you return to school or start on an undergraduate degree, you have to consider whether this tool is going to get you what you want. I don't believe that education for the sake of education is a good thing. You have to remember that higher education is a $95 billion institution that employs 800,000 instructors.[1] Like all institutions—be it the Elks, Colgate-Palmolive, or the Chamber of Commerce—higher education needs supporters to survive. Every time you or I take a course, we are supporting higher education—or our parents are.

What should you consider when you're looking through a school catalogue or listening to your boss encourage you to get a master's degree in computer science or public health administration?

One thing to look at is the cost. According to *U.S. News & World Report*, it now takes a middle-class parent ninety-five days of work to pay for a year at the average private college—versus forty-seven days twenty years ago.[2] Three years of film school can cost about $100,000.[3]

If you're working now, maybe your organization will pay for your education. Many organizations, including nonprofits, have educational benefits. If your organization doesn't offer tuition reimbursement, you might start searching for one that does. Moreover, those organizations that support further education frequently reward in some way those employees who go to school on their own time. That reward may range from praise to a promotion.

Going for a degree, particularly a graduate or professional degree, also represents an intensive commitment of time and energy. To succeed, you have to be pretty single-minded. That "well-rounded" life you were encouraged to have usually gets put on hold. If you have a family, they could suffer. You also have to ask yourself: Will going for a degree hurt my performance on the job? At a petroleum company there was a man in public affairs who went at night for his law degree. During the day he was irritable with coworkers. That hurt his image.

Also, you probably know friends with a degree from an Ivy League school who are working as waitresses or housepainters. The Bureau of Labor Statistics reports that one in five college graduates were doing jobs that didn't require a college degree. In addition, their pay stagnated.[4] In almost every profession there's a glut of educated people.

However, education gives you the tools to analyze possibilities in your line of work. The educated waitress may use waitressing not just to pay the rent but to learn the food business. From there she might go on to open her own restaurant or catering business. Or she can train to become a chef—one of the favorite occupations of your generation. She can also become a special events person at the Marriott or run all the food facilities at a hotel chain in Paris.

The educated housepainter could open his own housepainting firm. From what he learns about buildings, he also could train to become a real estate agent. In addition, there's the possibility of opening a store specializing in designer housepaints. He could work his way up to be vice president in an organization that markets paint.

Given economic conditions, there may be reasons to start out in a so-called dead-end job. However, because of your education, you can change your circumstances. How many college-educated secretaries worked their way up the ladder in public relations and advertising agencies? Education is the alchemy of the twenty-first century. That is, it can turn just about anything into gold.

What can you expect from higher education, and how can you get the most out of it? To help give perspective to the educational experience I've consulted with Jack Keane, the dean of the Business School at the University of Notre Dame. Before becoming dean, Jack Keane worked for thirty-six years in business and government. I think he has some unique insights about academia.

* * *

INTERVIEW: JACK KEANE

RLD: Jack, there are a lot of confused people out there when it comes to higher education. And that includes me. Someday I'll be sending my two sons to college, and I honestly don't know what to tell them "to do" there. Should they really hit the books, or should they start a business from their dorm rooms?

JK: They should always hit the books. But there's much more to college. When many of us think back to our university experience, we tend to feel that we underutilized it. We realize later in life that we didn't take advantage of all the opportunities the university had to offer. Just look at diversity, for just one example. So many different types of people entered our lives in the university. What an opportunity there was to get to know them better and to see the world through their eyes! Firsthand we could have learned how an Egyptian or French person thought. But how many of us went out of our way to take advantage of the opportunity? This is the sort of thing students should be alert to when they come to campus.

RLD: Why don't students take full advantage of what's there?

JK: The major reason is immaturity. The brightest, most talented, aesthetically oriented students can be immature and not take advantage of opportunities. On the other hand, those students who do take full advantage of opportunities are what I call the "great" students. They might not be the brightest or most talented, but they persevere. They inhale all that the classroom and campus have to offer. They're completely open systems. And they're able to experience everything going on. They judge the value of education after—not before—they experience it.

RLD: So immaturity can make a person less receptive to new learning?

JK: Correct. And in this Information Age, there's a continual need for new learning—of all kinds. It starts with formal learning in the classroom. Oh, there are extraordinary individuals who can bypass the classroom. They are the Bill Gateses of the world who seem to just sense what they need to know—and where to find it. But would even they not be better off had they possessed the full college experience?

RLD: So the classroom is just the start. There are also a million other ways to be learning on campus, aren't there?

JK: Things are moving so quickly you have to take advantage of all learning opportunities, including others outside the classroom. They include listening to visiting speakers, joining a theater group, writing for the campus paper, attending recitals and art exhibits, and going overseas.

RLD: For me, formal learning was divided into undergraduate and graduate school. Could we look at both of these? To begin with, what's the purpose of undergraduate school?

JK: There is no one purpose for getting an undergraduate degree. There are many. As I see it, it's important in the undergraduate years to give serious thought to what your life is about and how you're going to live it, plus the kind of person you wish to be. Within that context, then, you can pursue how you're going to make a living. You can also pursue the larger question of how you're going to make it a better world.

RLD: What should be the students' priorities in the undergraduate years?

JK: Students have to mature as much as they can. By "mature" I mean making the transition from a high school persona to adulthood. That entails getting a sense of purpose, accepting responsibility, and acquiring a sense of worth, plus a sensitivity about others— and, if you're fortunate, a willingness to help the less fortunate in consequential ways.

Another priority, of course, is to study. But, again, that doesn't only mean absorbing information from books. It also means being able to see the world through other people's points of view. According to a study by the Hudson Institute, by the year 2000 the majority of new entrants to the workplace are going to be women and minorities. In the workplace you are expected to deal with this diversity, including the disabled.

Another key priority is to be the best person you can be. College isn't just getting a degree. There's a bigger picture.

RLD: What are the pitfalls along the way? Why don't some students become, as they say, "all that they can be"?

JK: Some drift off in the wrong direction. When we sense this at Notre Dame, our first response is supportively to find out why. Sometimes that doesn't work. Some people are in denial and just want to pursue an unproductive lifestyle. But many others respond to our interest in them. We appeal to the idea that there are so many opportunities available in the undergraduate years and that they're cheating themselves if they miss out. When we approach students in trouble, we do so gingerly, because at first we may not know the hidden pressures on them. We also try to intervene early so that we can address the problems and handle them at a less serious stage.

Another pitfall is excessive socializing. Some students just get caught up in the social environment. That may be true where there are frats and sororities. Frats and sororities certainly have their place in college life, but their social function can be abused. Notre Dame doesn't have frats or sororities, but we still see students who neglect other parts of the college experience and focus too much on having fun—or immediate gratification at the expense of their long-range well-being. Again, it seems a matter of maturity and focus as to whether or not a student succumbs.

Another problem is family difficulties. They can certainly derail students. A divorce, illness in the family, a death, maybe finances—all can and do distract students. When confronted by such dilemmas, sometimes students simply need to drop out of school and regroup before reenrolling.

RLD: In terms of a future career, we all know that we should be studying hard. Every profession has a body of knowledge to be mastered. But how else can students prepare themselves for a specific profession?

JK: A key part of the college experience is internships. Students should choose the ones which are going to do them the most good rather than be the most fun. For example, it might be great to intern as a lifeguard over the summer, but that might not have great relevance to your career plans. There are all sorts of settings for internships. Students can intern at homeless shelters, businesses—large and small—and government agencies. The more diverse their experience, the better they're equipped to go out into today's work world.

So far in my career I've worked in ten different organizations spanning business, government, and academia. Being a part of such different worlds helped me to see different points of view. If students have well-rounded internship experiences, they will spot things in the environment which other people might not. That can give them the competitive advantage and enrich their understanding of the world.

Interning provides both students and companies a valuable opportunity to "test market" each other before making longer-term commitments. This makes for a win-win situation.

Career preparation also means networking. The people whom students get to know well on campus can be part of a lifelong network, both professionally and socially. One especially major mistake graduates make is not to keep those network contacts up.

RLD: Colleagues sheepishly tell me that their children have dropped out of college. I wonder why the embarrassment. Aren't there valid reasons for leaving campus—for a while?

JK: Well, there are definite signs that students are not taking advantage of the undergraduate opportunity. The biggest tipoff is that they start skipping classes. They might have lost a sense of direction—have no idea what they're doing in college. Family circumstances such as a death may have impaired their ability to function. Or they may have taken refuge in the party scene.

Some have failed to make friends and feel "alone in the crowd."

When we sense students are floundering, we give advice. Some don't want to hear it. They see themselves as doing fine. If students are wasting their time and money and can't seem to turn it around, we might ask them to leave the program and university for a while. We recommend that they take some time away to rectify the problem, with or without help.

RLD: How do students who have dropped out know that they're ready to return to college?

JK: Students who have dropped out should consider taking a course at a local college or university which is a worthy challenge to them. While they are taking that course, they should ask themselves if they're more attentive and if their studies are more interesting than they were before. If so, then students should take a few more courses. The goals here are to get back in the studying mode, gain academic momentum, and build confidence.

If students have come to enjoy the learning experience, then they might consider returning to the institution they were formerly enrolled in, unless that was part of the problem. They might decide to start out again someplace else. But they should be fairly certain that they want to resume studying, because, as you said, it can be embarrassing to drop out—once. It can be even more embarrassing to drop out twice. However, this experience needn't be embarrassing. Students who drop out should not think of themselves as failures but as wise persons who know they weren't ready for the college experience. Dropping out is not a stigma if done for worthwhile reasons.

RLD: Is the transition from college to the so-called real world difficult?

JK: Yes, it can be. My experience, however, is that it is not for most students. Most students have their eye set on a career goal. For instance, they may major in accounting. During the four years they apply themselves, they do well, and after graduation they enter their chosen profession. That's it.

Some students do have trouble with the transition. There are a number of factors involved. One, they might have studied what parents pushed them to study rather than what they wished to study. Or their head told them to major in X, but their heart wanted them to major in Y. This might pose a career dilemma, either on the first job or later in a career.

Also, some students can't seem to get into the rhythm of a job. In school they might not have done enough to get ready for the work world. The change is too abrupt for them, and they can't adjust.

To prepare for leaving school, there are any number of disciplined activities that they can do. For instance, at a job you have to show up at a predetermined time every day. At college, you can make it a point to get up at 7 A.M. every morning and start your day then, even though you might not have a class. George Burns cryptically observed that the first thing you need to do to succeed is to get up in the morning. Sounds so simple, yet so ignored.

RLD: What is the purpose of professional or graduate school?

JK: First let me say that the line between professional or graduate school is blurred. Sometimes professional schools are also graduate schools. The purpose of professional school or graduate school is to focus narrowly on a subject, such as medicine or American studies, in order to become a practitioner, teacher, or researcher. The need for this education is clear. Students recognize that they couldn't pursue a specialization without this education.

RLD: When's the best time to go to professional or graduate school—right after college or after a few years of work?

JK: Initially, I'll confine my answer to business schools. It's almost imperative to go to work for a few years. Most twenty-two-year-old graduates of college can academically do the work of business school. But they have no work experiences to contribute to the class. This point deserves attention. Business school is highly interactive, with your instructors and with each other. If you haven't worked a few years in, say, human resources or marketing, you have nothing to share. Therefore you also have little to bring to the group when you work as a problem-solving team on projects.

In schools of medicine and law, on the other hand, it might be appropriate to enter right after college. There, you're primarily interested in a body of knowledge, not experiences.

RLD: What are the pitfalls of going to professional or graduate school? For instance, can someone become a perpetual student?

JK: Honestly, I don't see a lot of perpetual students around. At least not at Notre Dame; Students here move in, move through, and move on. Besides, there isn't the money to support continuously going to school or stretching out the academic programs here.

RLD: Is there a downside to going to professional or graduate school?

JK: One potential peril of professional or graduate school is standing up to the competition. The competition to get in is strong. The competition to stay in is strong. And the competition to graduate well is strong. Everything is stepped up a notch from undergraduate school. Some will not measure up, and flunk out, resulting in wasted tuition money and eroded self-esteem.

RLD: Going to the right school is important. How can students select the right school for themselves?

JK: Go visit identified schools and live like a student. At Notre Dame, for instance, it's possible to come here for a few days, go to the dining halls, attend classes, and enter bull sessions. Instead of depending on a glossy brochure or online materials, you can see for yourself the size of the classes, the nature of the students, faculty and facility quality, the use of technology, and so on. Then basically ask yourself two questions: (1) Would I be comfortable here? (2) Would I be competent when I left?

RLD: How can students tell that professional or graduate school isn't for them once they're there?

JK: The biggest tipoff is grades. Bad grades are a definite signal of trouble. Also, the professors might be calling you in to speak with you about your performance. An earlier tipoff is recurring class cutting. Cutting classes is the best indicator of pending academic difficulties, regardless of the underlying causes. Some unhappy students sleep a lot or get out of the normal rhythm of living— perhaps staying up all night and sleeping all day. All this should tell you that school isn't for you—at least not right now.

RLD: Is professional or graduate school worth getting into debt for?

JK: You bet. And here I'm not talking about those studies which show that for each year of school you can earn so much money. What I am talking about are professional satisfaction and personal satisfaction. The educational experience equips you for a broader career. It's another arrow in your quiver, a competitive advantage in the marketplace. Also, you can—and should—make many good contacts in professional or graduate school. Your professional and personal satisfaction can be higher because you've been to a graduate or professional school.

RLD: Has professional school ever hurt anyone's career?

JK: It can happen—particularly in the short term. For example, you might be a shooting star within your organization. Then you tell them that you are leaving your job to attend a professional school full-time. They try to talk you out of it. When they can't persuade you to stay, they may become annoyed with you. After you finish school and your future employer does a reference check, they might call your previous employer and be given an unfavorable, and unfair review. While such decisions must be considered and made on an individual basis, my general view is to encourage graduate school. It certainly paid great dividends in my life.

RLD: When I went to graduate school at Ohio State I went full-time. Do you advise students to go full-time or part-time?

JK: That depends. Ideally, it's good to go full-time because you're not distracted by a job. But realistically, of course, that's impossible for many. Going part-time is better than not going at all. For example, at Notre Dame we have the Executive MBA Program for professionals who can't leave their jobs. They come to class on Fridays and Saturdays for two academic years. This type of program is a definite plus for them. For example, it helps them manage their time more effectively.

* * *

TAKING CONTROL

From what Dean Keane says and from my own educational experiences, it seems that to make your investment pay off you have to gain control over the educational process. You shouldn't just go to class every day and think you're getting an education. You have to be proactive about your personal and professional development.

How can you take control?

Part of that goes back to self-knowledge. Before you embark on an educational program, you have to know who you are and what you want from school. If you don't know that, then try it, as Dean Keane says, one course at a time. Had the writer Mary Jane Genova taken a few law courses part-time before going off to Harvard Law, she would have realized that law wasn't the field for her. But she went for the whole enchilada and wasted money and time.

You don't always have to dive off the big board. I've seen my share of belly flops. If you don't know what you want, try out different things. Put one toe in the water.

Also, you must do your homework—before you enroll. If you're considering a master's degree in field X or Y, go to practioners in those fields and ask them candidly what a graduate degree will get you in the work world. A woman I know was thinking about getting a master's degree in social work in order to write about such topics as eating disorders. When she spoke to social workers and psychologists, she found out that she didn't need that particular credential. What she did need was a track record or experience writing on mental health issues. They also suggested that she collaborate with practioners in the field. Those working in the field probably would be happy to have access to her writing skills, and she would benefit by having access to their knowledge base and experience. Higher education is not always the most efficient route to career change or enhancement.

While in school, you can't just retreat into the student life. You must keep in touch with practioners in the field to monitor what's going on in that field and then determine how that affects your educational choices. There was a super student at the University of Michigan who specialized in literary criticism. When she put herself on the job market for a tenure-track teaching position in literary criticism, she found out that very few institutions needed that expertise. At that time, the early 1970s, they were more interested in women's and American studies. Never get so engrossed in your studies that you lose touch with the outside world.

If you're attending classes while working full-time, that entails ongoing decision making. Day after day there will be time conflicts. You have to be clear what your priorities are. Do you just want a degree in communications, or do you also want high grades in your remaining courses? Often you don't need both. Some Tuesday you might have to decide whether to go to class or remain at work to help out with an emergency project. In my book, school should enhance your job performance, not interfere with it. In some disciplines, such as law, grades count for a great deal. In other disciplines, what you learn and how you apply that learning is more important.

Are courses you're taking in the evening or in the Executive MBA Program so demanding that you can't network? One evening business program had wine-and-cheese parties for students to network. Those get-togethers were as important to their careers as understanding a balance sheet. Strong bonds are made in educational programs. You have to make time to connect.

Things to Remember

- Higher education is the engine of the Information Age.
- Higher education is an expensive investment, both in money and time.
- You have to be proactive in getting an education.
- Don't let your education interfere with your job performance or networking.

11

YOUR WORK AND
YOUR PERSONAL LIFE

This chapter is must reading IF:

- You want more in your life than just work
- You're ambitious and worry that taking advantage of flexible programs can hurt your career
- You wonder why organizations have begun to help employees balance their work and personal lives
- Your parents were 100 percent dedicated to the organization and wound up being betrayed, and you don't want to repeat their mistakes

At work, you've probably been hearing a great deal about family-friendly policies. From those policies have come programs that help employees balance work and family life. Some of those programs are flextime, job sharing, telecommuting, onsite child care programs, and day care for the elderly.

You probably have some questions about those policies and programs. For example, you might be wondering:

- Does all this flexibility come penalty-free? Suppose your boss allows you to leave at 4:45 P.M. to pick up your infant daughter at day care. Will your boss hold this against you when it comes to bonuses and promotions? And if she does, is there anything you can do about it?

- Your parents used to talk about how rigid organizations were. It really was a nine-to-five world. Why are organizations changing? Is it in their self-interest to help employees balance their lives?

- Your wife expects you to do chores around the house. Yet you work long hours, and you're thinking of going to law school at night. Can those "balance" programs help you out?

In this chapter I'll look at these issues. First I'll interview Sheila Wellington, president of Catalyst. Catalyst is a nonprofit organization that helps business and public policy leaders focus on women's workplace concerns (although the organization recognizes that working men are now struggling with many of the same issues as are working women).

* * *

INTERVIEW: SHEILA WELLINGTON

RLD: Why are we hearing so much about the balance of work and family life?

SW: We are hearing so much about this because of a dramatic change which has taken place in recent decades. That change is the unprecedented number of women entering the workforce and remaining in the workforce. As recently as a generation ago, women entered the workforce and remained only until they married or had children. Today, studies show that about 70 percent of pregnant working women return to the employer within six months after giving birth to a child. With so many women in the workforce, obviously the balance issue becomes important.

RLD: We speak a great deal about the "issue" or "issues" connected with balance of work and family life. What exactly are those issues?

SW: Many studies document the fact that women, even when they have jobs, still bear the major responsibility for home and family duties. In general, less of the burden falls on men. Thus women are in the work world from at least nine to five, then enter another type of work from five to midnight. Women face tremendous pressure both in the workplace and at home. For a number of women, time has become more precious than money. Both organizations and women have had to look at all this.

In addition, another issue has emerged. Studies show that men are increasingly becoming concerned about the balance of their work and personal life. Therefore, balance is no longer simply a woman's concern.

RLD: How do you think that these issues will look in the year 2000?

SW: There will be more programs at more businesses. And those programs in place at that time will have more depth, more options, and be more widely used by employees. That's my prediction.

Right now we're seeing an increasing number of organizations offering flexible programs as a way to respond to the employees. That's because organizations are finding out that flexible programs reduce turnover and make it easier to recruit and retain both women and men.

It's interesting to note that ten years ago the Catalyst award for the most imaginative work/family programs went to initiatives that today would be considered quite common. About 60 percent of American corporations now have some kind of flexible work option.

RLD: If organizations don't resolve these issues, who gets hurt?

SW: It's the organizations that get hurt. Organizations that are lagging behind in providing flexible policies are finding it harder to recruit and retain good people. They also experience morale problems. And the longer they wait to introduce programs, the more difficult it will be for them to catch up.

RLD: Much of what I'm reading about these issues seems to put the burden of reform on organizations. Do employees have a role or responsibility in keeping their lives balanced?

SW: Yes, it's a shared burden. In terms of the organization, it must establish programs. Those programs must be in writing, and each feature must be made explicit. Also, they must be penalty-free. That is, employees shouldn't be punished for using the programs. For example, employees shouldn't be considered less committed to the job because they attend their son's Little League game.

As for employees, they must be flexible in terms of the needs of the organization. An employee may work a four-day week. Then there is an emergency project. Employees must consider those needs of the organization and be ready to adjust their schedules. It might be necessary for them to work a five-day week for a day or two. As you can see, flexibility must come from both the organization and employee.

RLD: Suppose your particular boss isn't enlightened about balance issues?

SW: Before you take the job, you have to be clear with your superiors about what your needs are, and you have to ask them if they can accommodate those needs. If you're already on the job, you might find that you get new bosses, and they don't seem to support flexible policies. Well, you don't know that until you discuss your needs. Also, you can explain that it is usually in the organization's self-interest to help employees balance their lives. Study after study shows this.

RLD: How can young people find out which organizations are sensitive to employees' needs?

SW: To begin with, there are the Catalyst award winners, which have been recognized for their outstanding initiatives to advance women. Young people can look into those organizations. Catalyst also publishes a popular guide about family-friendly workplaces. In addition, magazines such as *Working Mother* publish lists of organizations they've researched and recommend.

RLD: How can young people make a difference in regard to this issue? As you've said, it's an important issue, and I know there are young people who want to help shape how it's resolved.

SW: Young people can make a difference by making it clear what their needs are and thinking carefully about what jobs they take. This is especially true for young women. Studies show a tremendous volatility among managerial women in the workplace. In their current jobs they frequently can't find balance. So they often leave the organization. They go to another organization, which they hope is more flexible, or they start their own business. Why didn't they make their needs known? Had they done that, it might have changed the outcome. Of course, if a company cannot or will not adapt, then an exit may be the best option.

RLD: What's the cost of these policies?

SW: Right now there are no national studies on cost, but scattered studies and observations indicate that organizations save through these programs. Just look at turnover. Each employee who leaves because of a lack of balance costs the organization 95 to 150 percent of a year's salary.

* * *

THE ORGANIZATION MAN

The world of work that Sheila Wellington describes is very different from the world I entered in the 1960s. As she said, a generation ago most women didn't remain in the workforce. And we men had very little choice in how we handled our lives—both work and personal.

The choices or flexibility many of you now have in the workplace are relatively new. Since the end of World War II until about ten or fifteen years ago, there was an "organization man" mentality in America. Men went to work in large organizations. That's where the opportunities were. In return for access to those opportunities, the men conformed to the dictates of the organization. That might have meant wearing a hat to work. It might have meant not leaving the office in the evening until the boss left. It might have meant living in the suburb the organization wanted you to live in.

The organization men sacrificed just about everything to the job. If that meant working fourteen hours a day and missing their children's birthday parties, they did that. Although they might have been bone tired, they still were willing to go for drinks with colleagues after work, if that's what the organization expected. If there was a rush project, their families might not see them for weeks. In return for this intense loyalty to the organization, they were relatively well paid and had a shot at perks and promotions.

In his famous book *Organization Man*, William Whyte Jr. said that in the world of the organization man, "work...is dominant. Everything else is subordinate.... Whatever the segment of it [his life]—leisure, home, friends—he instinctively measures it in terms of how well it meshes with his work."[1]

I was an organization man for years. Believe it or not, it had its good points. Being part of a large, well-known organization gave me an identity. And there was no ambiguity—the rules were very clear. It never dawned on me to question those rules or to ask for a few months off to climb a mountain. My boss would have doubted my commitment—and my sanity. But as the economy, society and I changed, being an organization man became an increasingly bad fit for me. As Sheila Wellington emphasized, I was not alone. Everywhere, an increasing number of men are demanding more balance in their lives. And so are working women.

THE POST–ORGANIZATION MAN'S WORLD

Because of those changes, the organization man is becoming a dinosaur. New policies are emerging.

- In 1993, President Clinton signed the Family and Medical Leave Act. According to it, employees are supposed to get 12 penalty-free weeks off without pay for the birth or adoption of a child, to care for a seriously ill family member or to recover from a serious illness.

- According to the benefits consulting firm Hewitt Associates, within the past fifteen years 40 percent of large employers have started referral programs for child care, and 77 percent for elder care.[2]

- The accounting firm of Deloitte & Touche instituted reduced hours for partners and the opportunity to be made partner while on a part-time schedule.[3] This has helped women with children become partners more easily.

- A survey conducted by the insurance company CIGNA found that 41 percent of its male employees use at least one of the work/family benefits available.[4]

- First Tennessee Bank introduced flexible scheduling in its account processing department to help juggle the demands of work and personal life.[5] At one time banks and other financial institutions tended to be known for their rigidity.

There are a number of factors driving this revolution in the workplace. One factor is the change in the nature of work. With global competition and downsizing, employees are now expected to be more productive, creative, and accountable. Usually that entails putting in more hours. More hours mean that the day care center that operates from 8:30 A.M. to 5:30 P.M. is no longer adequate. More hours also mean more stress. Employees have to learn to deal with that. Also, more hours mean there's no one at home to let in the plumber.

Increasingly, employees are finding it difficult to cope with the new realities. As a result they're taking "radical" steps to restore some balance and reduce stress. For example, Juliet Schor, author of *The Overworked American*, surveyed a thousand people and found that 28 percent had made a change in their employment that lowered their earnings. Some moved to a less stressful job. Some turned down a promotion. Some refused to relocate.[6] A growing number of organizations have decided that they are going to be part of the solution for this problem. Those that aren't are getting bad reputations for being family-unfriendly.

Another factor is more women in the workforce. Currently, more than 40 percent of America's 60 million working women are mothers.[7] The dual-career household has become standard, putting pressure on men to do more around the house. Who takes the child to the 3 P.M. dental appointment or roots at the soccer game?

Employees are partly looking to employers for answers. Gone are the days when you kept your personal life hidden from your employers. As Sheila Wellington stressed, the new mindset about employee relations is that helping employees cope is a shared responsibility. Both the organization and the employee are supposed to pitch in and find a solution.

There is also a change of consciousness about work. With downsizing and consolidation eliminating so many jobs, people are more hesitant to make work "everything." Many in the current workforce are the "betrayed." They made tremendous sacrifices on behalf of their employers and still wound up losing a job or a number of jobs. It is often difficult to find comparable jobs. Increasingly work is seen as a means—a way to support a lifestyle—not an end in itself.

In addition, many initiatives to balance work and family are inexpensive or free benefits, and offering them is a good thing to do.[8] It helps employees and provides the organization with a progressive image. They include seminars on stress and parenting, sharing jobs, flextime, and working at home.

Many organizations that have offered work/personal life benefits have had excellent results. One result is good public relations. For example, in 1996, the pharmaceutical company Merck received a lot of attention when *Working Woman* declared it one of the ten best companies for working mothers.[9] That has made it easier for Merck to recruit and retain good people. As you can see, having flexible programs is now a factor in helping organizations develop positive images.

Work/personal benefits are also a clear signal to employees that the organization cares. This is a much-needed signal at a time when organizations can no longer offer lifetime employment yet are still asking for outstanding performance.

Turnover, which is expensive, is frequently reduced. For example, after the insurance company Aetna introduced family-friendly policies, 91 percent of new mothers returned to work versus 70 percent before the benefits. That saved Aetna $2 million.[10] First Tennessee Bank established a policy allowing full-time employees to become part-time employees and keep their benefits. About 85 percent of full-timers who were considering quitting for personal reasons stayed with the organization.[11]

DuPont claims that it gets back $6.78 for every dollar it spends on child care referral services.[12] That shows the kind of payoffs organizations can get.

And from what I've observed, work/personal life policies help recreate some of the bonds that existed between employers and employees before downsizing. You might say that these policies are part of the new social contract between employer and employee. When bosses let you work at home, saving you a two-hour commute, you're going to feel well-disposed toward them.

THE PITFALLS

No, some organizations have not kept their policies current with the new economic and social realities, says Paula Rayman, director of the Public Policy Institute at Radcliff College. There is urgency in the situation, she adds, because workers have accommodated as much as they can accommodate.[13]

One reason some organizations are finding it difficult to address those issues is that it requires a change of mindset. A tremendous one.

For example, employers must move from a point of view that employees must be carefully supervised to allowing employees to supervise many aspects of their own work, including how they use their time. Results or output must become more important than the time being put in. Also, the organization must be open to initiatives from employees. Employees might be able to reorganize work in such a way that it can be accomplished in three twelve-hour days rather than five, giving them more time for their personal lives.

You, too, must often change your mindset. You now have to be clear what you want from your career. You can no longer drift. If you want to be a vice president by time you're thirty—and it's possible—it might not be a good strategy to request switching from full-time to part-time work. There are always tradeoffs. If you become a part-timer and have more time for your personal life, you could be trading off a speedy ascent in the organization. If it takes a full-time employee ten years to qualify for partner, it might take a part-time one fifteen years.

In addition, flexible time does not mean less time devoted to the job. If you're at your son's first-grade graduation and work is heavy that day, you might think about coming in early or returning from the graduation and working late. Of course, you can also catch up with your work at home.

Another pitfall of work/personal life policies is the possible reper-cussions. Organizations never were and never will be perfect institu-tions, and there are considerable differences in how work/personal life policies are approached at different organizations or even in different departments of the same organization. For instance, one organization might have family-friendly policies on the books, but you will find that you are penalized if you use the policies. We probably all know stories about the women who took advantage of their organization's six-month maternity leave. When they returned, they found they were no longer on the fast track.

Perhaps your organization is very enlightened about helping em-ployees balance their lives. But it's a different story with your particular boss. He says you can work at home, but the next day you're back in the office he's abusive toward you. You get the message—and no longer work at home. Or you and your boss may be happy as clams with you working three days a week at home. However, your competition for a promotion has the ear of the boss all day, every day—and a chance to eat lunch with him those three days you are home. You have to take charge of your career. You must use common sense in evaluating the risks that go along with flexibility. The solution might be to keep coming into work every day until you win that promotion. After you become vice president, then you can decide whether you want to work at home and what the tradeoffs are. On the other hand, it could be that the organizational culture at work encourages working at home—and you could be penalized if you don't!

Check out how employees who have used policies you are interested in are faring. For instance, how are part-timers doing in their careers? Has their visibility gone down? Were any sidelined?

Or, if you want to become a partner in a law firm, you might work full-time until you achieve that status and then a few years later try to work out a less demanding schedule. In the new world of work, many things are negotiable that weren't negotiable just a decade ago. But frequently every case is approached differently. Just because Jim became partner and then cut back to thirty hours a week doesn't necessarily mean that you can do likewise. Jim may bring in $50 million of new business a year. Because he's a rainmaker, he gets special treatment.

Lesson number one in the balance issue: If you're applying for a job, take the time to find out what the real scoop is about the balance of work and personal life. If you're assigned to a new department or new boss, use networking to find out their positions on balancing work and personal life. At this time, not all organizations, departments or individuals realize that this issue matters to employees.

On the other hand, maybe this issue doesn't yet mean much to you. Maybe it'll never mean much. Then you don't have to rule out organizations that aren't helping employees juggle. Your career decisions are yours. Unlike in the days of the organization man, there is no longer one model for success. You may be very traditional in your work habits and still do very well in a number of organization. There are now almost infinite possibilities for configuring your career.

Things to Remember

- It's in organizations' self-interest to help employees balance work and personal life.
- You, too, have to be flexible, not just the organization.
- Not every organization is family-friendly.
- Evaluate the possible ramifications of switching to part-time or working at home. You are responsible for your career.
- This may not be an issue you're concerned about yet—or ever. There is no longer one model for success.

12

THE RIGHT THING TO DO

This chapter is must reading IF:

- You want to become more manners-literate
- You don't feel comfortable at professional lunches and other professional social functions
- You've offended a number of people
- You envy how self-assured some people are in your office
- You were a latchkey kid and no one seemed to have time to explain the social graces to you

Was the father of our country, George Washington, so successful because he was such a brilliant strategist or, as *U.S. News & World Report* says, because he had such good manners?[1] Probably a lot of both.

WHY HAVE GOOD MANNERS?

One immediate benefit of becoming more manners-literate is that you immediately become more sure of yourself. Old-money WASPs, who've always had excellent manners, also have always handled themselves with great self-assurance.

THE COMPETITIVE EDGE

Good manners have always been a way for up-and-comers to differentiate themselves from their competitors.

Two young men came to interview for a job at my firm recently. One had good manners. He acted like a guest and didn't get too comfortable. He said "please" and "thank you." And he demonstrated, by listening carefully, that he valued the time I was spending with him. The other young man seemed to be "above" manners. He slouched. He was a little too forward. He demanded, not requested, information from me. He got a little too comfy too fast. If I offer either one of them a job, it'll be the young man with manners. The other turned me off.

Good manners have helped me throughout my career. For example, one way I set myself apart from the competition is by hosting dinner parties for our key clients and prospects at my home. Doing this requires a lot of know-how in the social graces, even for my two young sons. My family and I are able to make an impression on the guests by practicing the laws of hospitality, laws that go back to the Middle Ages, laws that make guests feel welcome and special. For example, before a Japanese guest came over, I taught my son Geoffrey how to bow. Geoffrey practiced for days and was eager to do his thing. Well, my Japanese friend was so pleased by this gesture that he took the time to show Geoffrey how to improve his bow. The visit was a great success.

Right now, if you have good manners—even just so-so ones— you're ahead of the game. That's because, since the 1960s, many people have ignored manners. They don't know, for example, that they should walk their guest to the door, or not play a radio at work without asking coworkers if that's okay. In competing for new accounts, I can run rings around firms which are rough around the edges. Their rough spots say: *We don't know what we're doing. And because we don't, we're nervous.* As a result, people don't feel at ease around them. People love the self-assured. Self-assurance says: *I'm in control, and therefore I can help you.* My manners help clients have confidence in me.

THE BOTTOM LINE

Good manners not only get you in the door, they help an organization's bottom line. That's because good manners reflect respect for others and the wish to make them feel comfortable. In *Fortune*, Miss Manners (a.k.a Judith Martin) points out that if workers are not treating each other with respect, then you have to wonder how they're treating customers![2] Miss Manners is right. That's why organizations are hiring "manners consultants" to do everything from training the customer service staff to educating the staff in the new workplace mores. For instance, should you give a shower for a pregnant secretary who isn't married? Is it inappropriate to read faxes coming in for others?

A whole cottage industry has sprung up to take care of those matters of manners. Miss Manners, Letitia Baldrige, Barbara Pachter, Marjorie Brody, and others write thick books on the subject. Telephone Doctor Nancy Friedman's $2-million firm teaches phone etiquette.[3] Marjabelle Young Stewart trains executives in companies like AT&T and Merrill Lynch about manners.[4] If you are looking for an entrepreneurial activity, this is a growing field.

BONDING

Have you ever had a manager or client who treated you with respect and made sure you felt comfortable? Didn't that immediately establish a bond? I never forget those who treat me well. I go the distance for them. On the other hand, for those who treat me poorly, I just ignore them. No need to get even; the big world out there will chew them up and spit them out.

The world is unforgiving to the unmannerly. People have long memories for when they've been treated badly. Former astronaut Frank Borman found that out when he headed Eastern Airlines. His great image of being an American hero went out the window when he used bad manners, such as cursing. I wonder if New York Yankees owner George Steinbrenner would have had a less volatile career and established better relationships if he had good manners. An executive at a cosmetics company who was hosting a meeting of executives from around the country, including myself, alienated us all with a public temper tantrum. Because he was unhappy about how the food service had set up the room, he pulled the tablecloth and literally sent everything flying. It was a bad way to start off relationships.

HOW ARE YOUR MANNERS?

Here your generation might be at a disadvantage. The 1960s made manners seem like something the Establishment would dream up, which had no relevance to the new world of self-liberation. In fact, in many cases, bad manners, or no manners, were rewarded. For instance, if you told off a professor or someone else older than you, you were looked upon as a hero for "telling it like it is." If you were late to a dinner party, you weren't expected to apologize. And if you came empty-handed to that dinner party that was perfectly okay; because you probably didn't *feel* like bringing something. In those days, feelings were king, and you did what you felt like doing.

You probably also had both parents working, or a divorced single mom who worked. There probably wasn't anyone around to explain to you why it might not be wise to speak about religion or politics around the dinner table. And no one gently pointed out that your nonstop conversation about your home run in Little League might be boring people. So there may be a gap in your social education. But that gap can be easily filled.

BECOMING MANNERS = LITERATE

THE GOLDEN RULE

All manners are based on the Golden Rule. You treat others the way you want to be treated. Suppose you would like interviewers for jobs to let you get comfortable with them before they ask the "hard" questions, such as why you lost your last job. Well, that's exactly how you should treat those you interview at your office. Manners are not just a set of arbitrary rules that some manners expert made up.

Manners may seem like rigid rules, though, when they pertain to something you haven't experienced. For example, most manners books now have sections on how to do business in Asia or Europe. They'll tell you that in some Arab countries it is bad manners to expose the bottom of your shoe, and that in Japan you don't want to be the first to have tea. If you haven't traveled internationally on business, all that may seem silly, or as dry as dust.

But they aren't just rules to be memorized. When you follow the suggestions in the manners guides, you make your counterparts in the other country feel comfortable. And that's exactly how a well-mannered person wants to make another person feel. Any awkwardness puts your host in an uncomfortable position. If you don't bring your host in Japan a nice gift, for instance, that person will feel baffled because normal business protocol has been violated. That will create distance between the two of you. You don't want any unnecessary barriers getting in the way of the relationship.

In a Dale Carnegie seminar, students were asked not to use foul language. One lover of four-letter words buttonholed the instructor and said, "What are you guys, prudes? This is 1996." The instructor explained that bad language isn't recommended because it will offend many people. A well-mannered person doesn't want to offend *anyone*. A well-mannered person wants to be sensitive to other people's feelings—and most people aren't comfortable with four-letter words.

Think back to your last job interview. On that interview, did the interviewer have bad manners, like lighting up a cigarette without your permission or asking you your age (which is also not legal)? If you felt uncomfortable, you probably didn't perform as well as you could have. But good interviewers at good organizations, such as Procter & Gamble, have impeccable manners. That helps you soar when you present yourself for a job.

YOUR VALUES

Manners begin with your values. Would you help a colleague meet a deadline if he came into work, after a night on the town, at 11 A.M.? I don't know about you, but for me this situation—one in which the person brought trouble upon himself—wouldn't flash brightly on my compassion screen. I'd ignore the guy.

But perhaps your acquaintance down the hall is having trouble meeting a deadline because her boss suddenly died. She's been trying to get help through official channels, but with reengineering, everyone is overloaded. Would it be good manners to help her out as much as you can? Is that something you'd like someone to do for you? If it is, then it's good manners to help that person.

Do you believe that it's good manners to really listen when someone is talking to you? Then you'll listen, no matter what else is going on in your head. *Not* listening is the *height* of bad manners, at least in my book.

Make a list of your values. Then put an example next to each value, like this:

I'm compassionate. Therefore, I would feel sorry for someone who has no way to pick up his car at the service center. So I consider it good manners to give this person a ride if he comes to me and asks my help.

I'm competitive. Although I'm on a team, I still think that it's within the boundaries of good manners to call attention to my own achievements as long as how I do it doesn't detract from the accomplishments of the other players. I might send a memo to my boss pointing out what parts of the strategy were my ideas. I'd attach documentation such as memos I sent the team about those ideas.

Incidentally, in *Executive Etiquette in the New Workplace*, Marjabelle Young Stewart finds no breach of etiquette in team players differentiating themselves from the other players. Stewart says that when your interests don't coincide with the interests of the team, "it is important to know how to look out for yourself while maintaining a veneer of good manners." Your goal is to position yourself as a good team player while you gracefully promote yourself.[5]

I have a soft spot for the disabled, because my brother is disabled. In dealing with disabled people, I'll make sure they aren't ignored.

In *The Complete Business Etiquette Handbook*, Barbara Pachter and Marjorie Brody point out that it is good manners not to ignore the disabled. In addition, a well-mannered person will not use certain words with the disabled—such as "handicapped"—and will accommodate the disability. For example, if you were hard of hearing, well-mannered people would stand close to you and make sure you can see their lips.[6]

Take the time to examine your values. The best foundation for your manners is your own code of values. People will be able to identify you as an individual based on that code. That is one way you can differentiate yourself from others. Good manners, especially in these days of incivility, make you memorable.

RESEARCH

Your next step in becoming more manners-literate is to be willing to research the topic. Every library and every major bookstore has a section reserved for etiquette issues. On the shelves you will find books or "manuals" like *Business Protocol* and *Letitia Baldrige's New Complete Guide to Executive Manners*.[7] Just like a standard medical reference, one of those etiquette books should be on your shelf at home and in the office.

When you first pick up these books, they may seem like a formidable read. Wrong. The information, I've found, is truly amazing. There are so many aspects of human relationships that I never thought about in terms of manners. For example, how is the boss supposed to treat a secret office romance (that everyone knows about)?

Another way to research is electronically. I could go to the public library in Stamford, Connecticut, ask a librarian such as Irene Delor to show me how to operate InfoTrack, and come up with the latest thinking on manners. For free. I could retrieve *Barron's* article on Christmas gift-giving in the office, for instance. I would learn what gifts currently imply disrespect for people.[8]

I could also conduct online research—for a charge—through Dow Jones, CompuServe, and American Online. Through CompuServe, for example, I could retrieve an article from *Meetings & Conventions* on what's considered bad manners in 1995.[9]

Another way to do research is the oldest in the world: Ask someone's opinion. Suppose you share a secretary with eight other people. Over the past twelve months, she's only typed up one eight-page report for you. Should you give her a going-away gift? This is something you can talk over with someone else who understands the politics and manners of an office. Actually, you should talk it over with a number of people. And when you make a decision, it's best to err on the side of being generous.

THE NEW INCIVILITY IN BUSINESS

When you were applying for jobs recently, were you ticked off that some employers didn't even acknowledge your letter or inform you that the job was filled? Join the club. The professional world used to be known for its impeccable manners. If you applied for a job, you would hear from them promptly. And if you didn't get the job, they would send a personalized letter of regret. No more. Downsizing and reengineering have made many an organization seem a little rough around the edges. Their behavior lacks civility. According to *Fortune*, if you ask people why their corporate manners are so bad they would answer, "We're all too busy—and stressed."[10]

But when it comes down to individual human beings—when it comes down to *you*—no one gets off the hook. The people you offend will vividly remember your bad manners. So take the time to thank an assistant for staying late, or apologize to a colleague if you interrupt him at a meeting. Manners still count—a lot. When he was at Chrysler, finance executive Chris Steffen would always take the time to write a thank-you note to an employee and then carbon-copy the employee's superior. Steve Miller, a genius at putting together financial deals at Chrysler, made sure he would speak to your boss personally about how your work had benefited him. Dick Goeken, president of synthetic fuels at the former Gulf Oil, would not only see your boss but stop in and see you to express his appreciation directly. In today's organization Steffen, Miller, and Goeken might be the exceptions. But they would probably get better results from their people than managers without manners.

If you have bad manners, you'll pay. Bill Agee, chief executive officer at the former Bendix and then at Morrison-Knudsen, created the perception that he had bad manners. Bill is actually a very gracious man, but at Bendix he promoted Mary Cunningham, a woman he later married. Many in the organization thought it was bad form. Then, at Morrison-Knudsen, rumors got around that Agee didn't like Boise, Idaho, where the organization was located, and his decision to run the organization from California seemed to confirm the rumors. The troops considered that bad manners too. In both cases, Agee was hurt.

If you are among those handing out the unkind treatment, you will be hurt—and so will your organization. As Julie Conelly points out in *Fortune*, when employees deal roughly with each other, personality clashes become routine. That drains productivity." Today, bad manners is one of the biggest productivity killers in the work world. A subordinate who's spoken to abruptly by a superior could obsess about it for days, badmouth the boss on the grapevine, and make sure he's super frosty to the boss. All that drains time and energy from his work.

Some young people I know are taking extra time to be polite in the workplace. I see this strategy as paying off for them in a major way. People don't like to be treated poorly. They especially don't want to be treated poorly by someone younger than they are. Good manners build a good reputation for you throughout the company and your profession.

QUESTIONS OF MANNERS

In writing her books, Miss Manners didn't go up on a mountain like Moses and bring down two tablets with the Ten Commandments of manners. Rather, she and other experts look at their experiences, take into account the mores of the era, and describe how they would handle something. For you, though, the approach they recommend might not be right. Young people see the world in unique ways. You could probably produce a bestseller if you were to issue your own guide to manners for young people.

That book doesn't exist yet, so I've put together this section. It focuses on questions people in your generation have asked me about manners. I have tried to put myself in your shoes. If you disagree with my interpretations, I hope that you'll share your thinking with me.

Through the grapevine I've heard that my boss is getting fired. How should I act toward her?

Well, how would you like your subordinates to act toward you in this situation? You'd probably want to be treated with respect and sensitivity as long as you're the boss. You wouldn't appreciate people spreading the rumor that you're about to get canned. And when the ax did fall, you'd want subordinates to say they're sorry about the situation and to offer to help. Also, you would want people to speak well of you after you leave.

I wonder about the proper etiquette for e-mail.

Many of the same principles that pertain to written communication and phone calls pertain to e-mail. All of them involve consideration for the recipient. When I first started using e-mail, I fell in love with the process and contacted just about everyone I knew several times a day. Yes, I made a pest of myself. What I do now is ask myself, "Is this message necessary?" If it is, I send it. If not, I don't send it. I try to keep the message short, about one screen. And before I send it off, I ask someone in the office to proofread it. Having a typo in e-mail is as offensive as having one in a typed letter.

There I was at the fax machine, waiting for my fax from a client. Bored, I started to read another fax coming through. The woman who was receiving the fax really chewed me out. What did I do wrong?

Think about it: Would you like your colleagues reading faxes that came to you? No, of course not. Many faxes are semiconfidential. For example, if a colleague scanned a fax coming in to you, he might find out that your client didn't like your approach for the 25th anniversary celebration of his company. That kind of information is not something you want the whole office to have.

Can I send a memo to a client?

No. Memos are intended for internal distribution. When communicating with a client you would send a formal letter. Some firms do send memos to clients, but it's considered bad form.

I went to the most boring speech at the Chamber of Commerce. Isn't it good manners for the speaker to try to make the talk interesting?

Yes. Before preparing the speech, speakers should ask themselves: "What can I say to this audience that will make this half hour spent with me useful to them?" It's common courtesy not to waste other people's time. On the other hand, it's also good manners to appear interested in what the speaker has to say.

I have had lunch with people who make several calls during lunch on their cellular phone. Isn't that rude?

Yes. Such behavior is only permissible if the matter is urgent and the caller asks your permission to interrupt the lunch and make the call.

I had a job interview, and I didn't send a follow-up letter. I figured that I made all the points I wanted to make in the interview. But some people say I was wrong.

A follow-up letter is a good idea because it gives the organization feedback on how you perceived the job. It also signals that you're interested in the job. Some type the letter, some send the letter handwritten. Either way it should go through the mail, not by the fax—unless there is real urgency in the interviewing process, or they specifically ask you to get back to them by fax.

I don't know what to wear on casual day.

Proper attire on "casual" or "dress-down" day depends on the organizational culture. In some organizational cultures, blue jeans are okay. In others, people are more formal and wear slacks with a blazer. Look around the office and notice what the up-and-comers are wearing. That should be your guide.

I noticed that no one talked business at a company wine-and-cheese party. So I didn't either. Should I have said something about my work? My boss's boss was there.

Again, your behavior depends on the organizational culture. At many organizations it's considered gauche to discuss professional matters at a social function. At others, such as startup firms, *everything* involves business. And there are exceptions. At some organizations your boss might discuss an urgent professional matter with you at the Christmas party.

I have trouble with small talk. What's proper professional protocol?

Pachter and Brody point out that it's wise to keep small talk light and focused on topics that are of interest to everyone.[12] It's also important that small talk doesn't offend. For example, suppose you point out what's wrong with the Catholic religion. That could make the Catholics in the group feel uncomfortable or hurt. Listen in on other groups' conversations. Notice what they say and don't say.

Before you go to an event, make sure you are up to date on current events. Another guest might ask you what you thought of Colin Powell's speech at the Republican National Convention or the latest drop in the Dow Jones Average. The news makes small talk easier. It's also full of "safe" topics.

How should I conduct myself at a meeting?

Again, the organizational culture will dictate most of your behavior. For instance, at some organizations junior members aren't encouraged to talk at meetings. But no matter what the organizational culture, there is a basic etiquette for meetings.

Arrive on time and don't leave early. If that's not possible, don't disrupt the group with your comings and goings. Treat everyone's input with respect. Don't monopolize the conversation. Make sure your comments are helpful. People know when you're talking just to talk, and that wastes their time.

When you go to a professional lunch or dinner, how much actual professional material should be discussed?

As much as the *most* powerful person at the table wants. That person will also have the authority to decide when the professional discussion should begin. Follow that person's lead.

I'm always on a diet, so I order salads at professional lunches. Unfortunately, they're tough to eat. What should I do?

Salads *are* tough to eat. And if you're struggling with the salad, it's bound to make your colleagues at the table uncomfortable. Fortunately, there are other low-calorie, low-fat entrees that are less of a challenge. You might try fish or a cottage cheese plate.

If you are on a diet you can usually call ahead for the restaurant or hotel to have a special meal for you. This is becoming increasingly common. I usually let them know ahead of time that I want seafood without butter.

I sense you're damned in an office if you talk about your off-the-job social life, and damned if you don't. In the first instance, people have the dirt on you. In the latter case, people think you're secretive. What should I do?

It's a fact of professional life, say Pachter and Brody, that "you're judged by your hobbies, interests, and lifestyle."[13] Therefore, be discreet. The easiest way to judge what to disclose is to consider the organizational culture. In that organizational culture would it be okay to discuss a marathon weekend of sex? Before you reveal anything, put it through the organizational culture test. How would this information be viewed in this organization?

Also, remember that whatever you decide to disclose about yourself could have ramifications—good and bad—on your image. If you've spent the weekend fixing up houses in a low-income neighborhood, coworkers might perceive you as a good citizen, or as a bleeding heart liberal. Remember that not everyone shares your values.

It's also good manners not to make anyone at work uncomfortable about your lifestyle. If for any reason your lifestyle will upset others, keep it quiet.

Things to Remember

- Good manners give you the competitive edge.
- Manners are really about the Golden Rule.
- Your values determine your manners.
- People respond strongly to good manners—and bad manners.
- Spend some time researching manners.

13

AFTER A SETBACK

This chapter is must reading IF:
- You've ever had a setback
- You blame yourself entirely for that setback
- You're angry
- You're just plain scared

If you've already had a career setback, thank your lucky stars. That puts you ahead of the game. Give me several job candidates side by side, and I'm likely to choose the one who's had a few bumps in the road. That person tends to be more alert, tolerant, and pragmatic than a candidate who hasn't experienced the dark night of the soul. In *Nation's Business*, Michael Barrier points out that early setbacks help you sort out what success really is for you.[1] Had you not had that setback, you might be blindly following conventional wisdom about career paths or assuming your career strategies are invulnerable.

A setback also puts you in some very good company. Winston Churchill, Lee Iacocca, and Steve Jobs all suffered major setbacks and then went on to amazing triumphs. In *Churchill: A Study in Failure*, Robert James emphasizes that from 1929 through September 1939, Churchill held *no* public office, and many people perceived him as an utter failure. He then went on to become one of Great Britain's greatest war leaders.[2] Lee Iacocca was fired from Ford Motor

Company and was considered to be a dead issue in the automotive world. Then, in the late 1970s, he came back to lead the Chrysler turnaround and became a legend in his own time. Steve Jobs was ousted from Apple. His Next company never really got off the ground. But he returned to glory via his computer animation firm, Pixar.

Setbacks frequently are a transformational force. They can turn the average person into a tiger.

OPPORTUNITY

George Daly, who is dean of the Leonard N. Stern School of Business at New York University, deals with a lot of successful people. Most if not all of them, he says, suffered setbacks—and used that dark night of the soul as an opportunity. "Successful people," observes Dean Daly, "learn from their setbacks and become even more determined."

Today, because of the volatility of the global economy, we're seeing more and more setbacks. Back when I started my career, business was highly predictable. You went to work in a large organization and, unless you were a roaring incompetent, you climbed the ladder to increasing levels of money, prestige, and status. On the other hand, the few who managed to get themselves fired became pariahs. Being fired had a terrific stigma attached to it in those days. Fortunately, that is no longer the case.

Getting canned has become almost a rite of passage in this brave new world of global business. In addition, you're more apt to have failures on your watch—just read business publications. That new product or service doesn't work out. The reorganization you help orchestrate doesn't increase profits. Your management style irks some employees, they bail out, and the media starts talking about a brain drain at your company.

In short, if you're alive and working at this point in history, you're bound to have a setback. What matters is not the setback per se. It's how you work your way through it.

George Daly has some interesting insights on setbacks, especially since he worked through at least one himself. I have, too.

* * *

INTERVIEW: GEORGE DALY

RLD: In the circles where you travel, are you seeing more setbacks today?

GD: There's no question that there's more turbulence in business, and that tends to produce more setbacks. But I always argue: For every setback there's an *opportunity*.

RLD: Could you explain how setbacks can be opportunities?

GD: The key is to be able to learn from the setback. Not only *could* you learn from a setback—you *should* learn from it.

RLD: Do young people, because they're relatively new to the work world, tend to take a setback harder than a mature person?

GD: It depends. I think, on the average, yes. But there's a lot of variation. We can all remember when we were young and it seemed like the world was ending when we broke up with a girl. However, I also know some fairly senior people who have had setbacks, and some of them have reacted very poorly. I believe that a setback is often a kind of defining moment for people. It literally is sort of a test of character, and we see what the person is made of.

RLD: In an ideal world, how should young people react to a setback? Perhaps they came in second for a job, were passed over for promotion, or were let go in a downsizing.

GD: The first thing young people can do is let off steam: Get out there and talk about what happened. I think that the biggest problems occur with setbacks when we bottle up the whole thing within ourselves and don't talk to others. When you talk about it with others, you get some perspective. For example, you realize you're not the first person in the world to have a setback.

RLD: In addition to ventilating, what else should young people do?

GD: They need to reflect on what the experience means. A good example of this is the person who loses a job and is shocked; these people claim they didn't see the signals. This is significant and needs to be looked at.

In my line of work I have terminated a fair number of people. If they're shocked—if they didn't see it coming—then I consult with their superiors. I ask, "Was this person alerted to the fact that their performance wasn't adequate?" I check over the personnel record.

It has *never* happened that signals weren't sent. The person just didn't pick up on them. And that's why these people have to look at themselves. Why the tunnel vision? For this reason, we send those we dismiss to extensive outplacement counseling. During counseling they have the opportunity to examine how they see the world.

RLD: What about your personal experience with setbacks?

GD: I'm not atypical; I've had my share of setbacks. The one that comes to mind is the time when I was competing for a job. I *really* wanted that job. The search was narrowed down to a small group of finalists. Going into the last set of interviews, I might have been the favorite. And I felt that the last set of interviews had gone well. In fact, I went home thinking I had the job. Well, they chose someone else.

RLD: What did you do about that?

GD: I retraced my steps through the whole job interview process and took a look at how I presented myself versus how I perceived I was presenting myself. I contacted some members of the job search committee to give me feedback. As a result of that analysis, I think that I'm a more effective professional—and person.

RLD: Thanks for sharing that. My setback was a little different. I had been with a large organization for twenty-plus years. Then there were changes. I was forced to look at myself and ask if the corporate world was still for me. That took a lot of soul-searching. I was terrified of reconfiguring my career path. I was also angry that outside forces were pushing me towards change. So I did what Dwight Eisenhower used to do. When he was angry with someone, he put that name in a drawer. He let some time pass and then pulled out the name. Thanks to time, the name had lost its hold on him.

I ultimately decided not to get another job in another large corporation. What I really wanted was to try my hand at running my own business. Had I not had a setback, I would never have experienced the absolute high of being an entrepreneur. I would still have been in that old comfy corporate cocoon, and probably not growing. A setback delivers you a message that you *have* to pay attention to.

I was wondering: Can future setbacks be prevented?

GD: Absolutely not. Setbacks have always been with us, and always will be with us. With the volatility of the global marketplace, there will just be more of them. But that also means there will be more opportunities.

* * *

THE FAILURE TABOO

For many years America was not a good place in which to have a setback. As John Ward points out in *Song of the Phoenix: The Hidden Rewards of Failure*, our Calvinistic roots made us phobic about failure. That was for two reasons. One, the tenets of Calvinism held that God rewarded good people with material success. Therefore, if you weren't succeeding, you probably weren't a good person. The holiest person in church was the person with the most material goods. Two, according to Calvinism your profession was considered sacred. If you were an accountant or a nurse, that was as sacred a vocation as being a member of the clergy.³ This meant that everything that affected your profession was viewed in a very serious light.

Screwing up professionally thus had dire implications. Therefore, when we did screw up, we tended to try to keep it quiet. Talk about failure might be among the last taboos left in America. But when Lee Iacocca was introduced at a college lecture as "having left Ford and gone to Chrysler," Iacocca the iconoclast took on the failure taboo. He strode right to the podium and said, "I didn't leave Ford, I was fired." And he brought the house down.

In the media there are lots of stories of comebacks—but not too many articles about people when they're *struggling* to come back. In *Complete and Utter Failure*, Neil Steinberg observes that "those who fail, who come in second, whose sales figures disappoint" are quickly eliminated from our radar screens.⁴ We have tended not to deal with them anymore.

But all that has been changing. It had to. There are now just too many of us who fail, come in second, or disappoint. I prepare the staff in our agency—as I do my two sons—for failure as well as for success. And when I think about my successful colleagues and what they were doing over the past five years, there isn't one of them who hasn't had some kind of defeat.

I believe it was in the late 1980s, about the time downsizing became the new modus operandi of business, that the stigma associated with failure began to lose some of its power. Churches in posh suburbs like Westport, Connecticut, began to offer support groups for unemployed executives. Some of those executives allowed themselves to be interviewed by the media; they actually *talked* about being out of work. In 1987, Carole Hyatt and Linda Gottlieb's book *When Smart People Fail*, openly discussed failure and named names of those who had failed. The book's stance was not that if you failed, you were a bad person; instead, the authors contended that failure was the result of being in the wrong niche. The typical failure was the entrepreneurial type who was stuck in a buttoned-down organization—and not doing well. Recently I did an online business literature search for the word "failure" in the title. About 1,035 entries appeared.

Failure is not just out of the closet; it's now coming to be perceived as a character builder. For example, observers who comment on the strengths of your generation, such as Karen Richie, look at the setbacks you've had to overcome—ranging from your parents' divorce to the holding power of the stagnant economy.[5] Their conclusion is that your adversity has been your blessing. Your adversity, for example, has forced you to network.

Clearly, failure has become more acceptable. The question is: Are you willing to *accept* your failures?

MAKING SETBACKS WORK FOR YOU

How can you tap into the power of a setback—and make it work for you? I have nine recommendations.

If you're shocked by the setback, ask yourself why. In *Ambition: How We Manage Success and Failure Throughout Our Lives*, Gilbert Brim observes that "sometimes we don't know we are losing until the very end."[6] And that's not entirely our fault. In a nation of optimists, there's reluctance to deliver bad news. It's the courageous supervisor—and the equally courageous colleague—who will even hint that there are major problems. Oh, certainly, there are signals: Your work comes back from the new powers-that-be with plenty of red pencil, and something in your gut says the new regime and you aren't on the same wavelength. But it's not unusual for the brass not to spell out that there's a problem. When it comes to bad news, your colleagues are usually equally evasive. Then one day, seemingly out of the blue, someone in command says, "This just isn't working out."

You can avoid the shock, and perhaps even prevent the setback from happening, if you develop the ability and the willingness to read the text beneath the surface. It's best to consider *everything* in the workplace as symbolic. If you're not invited to a meeting, ask yourself what that means. If you don't receive a raise, ask what that could represent. If the bosses are consistently impatient with you and act like you really get under their skin, ask yourself what might be going on.

If this looming setback can't be prevented, don't waste time in denial. Your first few phone calls should be to those who've gone through similar ordeals. Those kinds of conversations bring home to you that you're not unique and that, yes people do survive your particular kind of setback. Even before the setback occurs, start thinking about how to deal with it from a position of strength. Certainly, you might want to consult a lawyer. But think seriously about all your options.

Be gentle with yourself. Jean Pope, an instructor in technology and society at the Heald Institute in San Francisco, advises young people that there's a place for them in the work world and that they should continue to believe in themselves. When I spoke with Pope, she said, "Young people have to consider the times we live in. It's like everything is up in the air. And we're waiting for the dust to settle."

Don't take full blame for the setback. John Lord points out that usually the total responsibility for the problem isn't yours.[7] For example, suppose you left a good job in sales in order to train to become a medical doctor. You then flunk out of medical school. In that case, a counselor like Lord would tell you to analyze how society might have influenced your choice. Then you might see that medicine, even in this era of managed care, has more prestige in some people's eyes than sales does and that you were simply vulnerable to this type of professional pressure. Also, you have to ask who else owns a piece of the problem: Who encouraged you? Who in your sales organization precipitated your dissatisfaction? Should the medical school have warned you that you might have difficulties returning to school at your age?

It is pure grandiosity to claim total responsibility for any setback. The credit is never all ours when we win, and the fault is never 100 percent ours when we lose, either.

Get feedback. At the very least, doing this will let you know what people might be saying about you. And because you're in a crisis, you'll find that people will tend to be straight with you.

After she was selected for the first wave of layoffs at a major food company, a writer did a smart thing. She went to one of her colleagues in the public relations department and asked why she had been selected to go in the first wave. She knew there was a message there but just didn't know exactly what it was. The colleague was candid and told her she was a poor fit for corporate life. "But," said the writer, "I have never had trouble with senior management. And aren't they the ones who count?" The colleague then gave her an education on how images are formed in an organization, pointing out that the reason the writer had gotten by with senior executives was probably because their interaction with her was so limited. "You can't sustain being a good corporate citizen" was the way the colleague summed up her situation. Believe it or not, this was the first inkling the writer had that perhaps she didn't belong in this type of organization. And, by leading her to a more hospitable work setting, this setback changed her life.

Be open to alternatives, even if they're not directly related to your current career path. A media representative who was laid off decided to try out her long-term dream of selling for a living. She realized that a lot of the skills she used in pitching stories to the media could be used in sales. She turned out to be more successful in sales than she had been in media relations.

Many layoffs occur because you are in a declining industry or a shrinking profession. Once you're out of it, the playing field seems more level, and you begin to do well.

Keep it simple. Much of the advice you get during this crisis might seem simplistic. And it is. On the other hand, your problem might seem very complex to you. But it probably isn't. One man was put on probation at his job and assumed it was because he had deep-seated problems with authority. A colleague let him in on a little secret: "You can't stand the boss, and it shows." The solution to the problem was not for the man to figure out why he hated the boss; it was simply for the man not to be so open in showing his feelings. If you think interpretations people give you for why you suffered a setback are simplistic, keep listening; they're probably just cutting through all the psychobabble we've picked up since the 1960s.

Move toward the future. The last place where you want to be stuck is with your current problem. That's why so many people get active after a setback. They want to see movement. They want change. They go on diets, learn new computer skills, travel to San Francisco to see if they would like to relocate there, develop a whole new network, start new exercise regimes. Activities like these allow their frame of reference to be *post*-setback.

Realize you're not the first person to be scared. You have plenty of company. Also, realize fear is usually our friend; it warns us to be careful. Fear becomes the enemy only when we allow it to control us. If you're becoming overly scared, call up someone who has been in your shoes and is now doing just fine.

Refrain from becoming preoccupied with setbacks. Sure, you'll learn a lot about failure when you're going through it. But your goal is to *go* through it and not be fixated with failure. It's just one part of your professional experience—hopefully a small part.

Things to Remember

- Setbacks can be opportunities.
- Don't isolate after a setback.
- Don't take full blame for the setback.
- Don't become preoccupied with a setback.

14

MENTORS

This chapter is a must read IF:

- You're wondering what a mentor is and whether you need one
- You're outgrowing your current mentor
- You suspect there's a downside to the whole "mentor" thing
- You don't know how to get a mentor
- You feel like you're alone
- You realize you need help

Mentorship has been getting a lot of press in the past few years. You can't open up a publication for your age group and *not* see an article about the pros and cons of having a mentor.

Fashion designer Bill Blass, Supreme Court Justice Sandra Day O'Connor, former surgeon general C. Everett Koop, and news anchor Charlayne Hunter-Gault all say that a mentor played a major role in their development.[1] They're not alone. In fact, virtually every successful person has had some kind of mentor. The mentor could have been Mom or Dad, the football coach, a math professor, an executive in the community, or chief executive officer of the company. In *The Mentor Connection*, Michael Zey cites a Heidrick and Struggles study of 1,250 senior executives whose names had appeared in the "Who's News" section of the *Wall Street Journal*. *Two-thirds* of them said that they had had a mentor—and of that two-thirds, a third had had *two or more* mentors.[2] And, not surprisingly, a number of you have told me that you need mentors.

In this chapter I'll discuss what mentoring is. I'll interview my former mentor, Walter Seifert, who taught communications for twenty-four years at Ohio State University and helped thousands of kids get jobs. I'll discuss the benefits and pitfalls of the mentoring process. And I'll give recommendations on how you can attract the right mentor for you.

WHAT IS A MENTOR?

What exactly is a mentor? That depends. Most mentors and protégés have their own ideas as to what mentoring is all about. In *Working Woman*, Kathy Kolbe points out that a mentor could simply be a person who serves as a role model, period. That person doesn't necessarily have to promote your advancement politically or even give you advice.[3] Rather, as you observe and analyze the person's behavior, you come to conclusions about what your behavior might be. On the other hand, Michael Zey has a more broad understanding of "mentor." Zey defines a mentor as someone who oversees someone else's career and development through "teaching, counseling, providing psychological support, protecting, and at times promoting or sponsoring" that person.[4]

At the beginning of the relationship, it's useful for you and the mentor to articulate what the parameters of the relationship will be. For example, you might be assuming there'll be political help when the mentor intends to restrict the relationship to meeting for lunch once a month and encouraging you. Also, the parameters might change during the relationship. Your mentor may become too busy to offer broad-based support anymore or may acquire a position of power and be able to help you politically. This relationship is fluid.

On the other hand, there are many mentoring relationships in which nothing is made explicit. The relationship just sort of happens, and neither you nor your mentors comment on the nature of the relationship.

MULTIPLE MENTORS

To get what you need, you might require two or more mentors. The mentor relationship isn't like marriage. It's not supposed to last for life. And it isn't monogamous; you can have two or more mentors at the same time. For a long time my mentor was my dad. Then I graduated from college and wasn't sure what I wanted to do. I found my number two mentor when I went to Ohio State for graduate school in communications. In addition to being an inspirational professor, Walter Seifert has been active in the profession. He started the Public Relations Student Society of America (PRSSA) in 1967. Then he went on to found the educators' section of the PRSSA and later was chosen as outstanding teacher by the organization. His writing has appeared in major newspapers, including *USA Today*. I still think of Seifert as one of my advisers.

* * *

INTERVIEW: WALTER SEIFERT

RLD: How would you define this entity we call "mentoring"?

WS: I think of mentoring in simple terms. It's helping another person succeed.

RLD: Do you think mentoring is necessary for success?

WS: As I look back over my own career and the careers of my best students, it certainly appears that they—and I—got more help from the outside than from within ourselves. For example, one of my big breaks came through a mentor.

I was working as the night editor for a newspaper syndicate in Cleveland called Central Press. During the day I would fish in Lake Erie. One day I caught half a bushel full of fish. I cleaned them and brought them into the syndicate. Everybody got some. Well, the editor came out of his office and said, "Mr. Seifert, I think you ought to write a fishing column." Thanks to him I wrote a fishing column that appeared in a hundred newspapers. It was called "Fish Tales." And "Fish Tales" got me a trip to Bermuda. I met my wife in Bermuda and got a job there as a director of public relations—all because someone took the time to guide me.

RLD: How did you get to Ohio State?

WS: The head of the journalism school wanted to introduce some public relations courses. Over twenty-four years, I've had 10,000 students. I think they wanted me because I had actually worked in the profession. And that's what a good mentor has to do—know the field from hands-on experience. Too many educators know their areas of expertise from books rather than experience.

RLD: What are the benefits of having a mentor?

WS: A mentor can tell you about a field because the mentor has had a deep relationship with that field. Also, the mentor can assess a person. The mentor can make a judgment whether the person has the horsepower for the field. In addition, if the mentor is like me, the mentor can help the young people get jobs in the field. I've been able to help a number of young people. But I'd place them only if they were strong in their field.

RLD: So you consider finding jobs for people part of your mentoring activities?

WS: Yes, at least the first job. That's the toughest to get. But I also considered it part of my role to discourage weak students from entering the field. I felt that that was also my responsibility.

RLD: Were there any negative fallouts from your mentoring?

WS: Probably the biggest was the disapproval of some of my teaching colleagues. Some saw my mentoring work with students as a waste of time.

RLD: I've heard horror stories about mentor relationships that go on too long. For instance, the protégé outgrows the mentor or becomes more successful than the mentor. Do some mentors hold on too long?

WS: Certainly. As far as I know, I haven't had that problem. I enjoy following someone's career, and often that's gone on for years. In fact, for fifteen years I had a newsletter called *Jewel Club Newsletter*. It was for all those I had mentored. In it I brought people up to date on everyone's accomplishments. Once a year, I ran a contest. Readers were to submit their best work, and the winners would get a prize.

If someone doesn't want to keep in touch with a mentor, though, that's something you can spot right away, and you leave that person alone. And there are points in someone's development when that person needs a different type of mentor. I use the analogy of medicine. Usually you start out with a general practitioner, but often you need a specialist. So you go from the generalist to the specialist, and you get what you need. As you rise in your profession, you'll get more sophisticated mentors who are on top of the field you're now in, or will be in.

RLD: How would you advise a young person to find a mentor?

WS: A bright young person should survey the environment and find out who can be of help. It's best to find local people. If, for example, you want to enter public relations, then you should survey those whom you know in public relations. When you've selected someone you want to approach, ask this person if he or she could answer a few questions for you. That could lead to a relationship, and even a job. If there are no public relations people you can talk to in your environment, then go to the library, look up the names of public relations people, and contact them with questions. See where that leads.

RLD: What do you get out of the mentoring relationship?

WS: Personally, I enjoy watching young people develop. Every time one of "my kids" has a success, I feel a tremendous degree of satisfaction. For example, Bob, when you publish a book I feel very happy for you.

RLD: Thanks, Walt. It was you who helped me get a sense of who I was and who I could be professionally. You also guided me to see what my strengths were. I couldn't believe you thought I had so many!

* * *

WHAT'S IN IT FOR YOU?

For me, Walter Seifert is the Mr. Chips of the mentoring world. But the benefits you get from mentoring might not include a Mr. Chips–type relationship. It might be much more businesslike, especially if your organization assigns you a mentor. A number of organizations now provide high-potential people with mentors. Your mentor may tell it exactly like it is and not be sensitive to your feelings. There's no one model for what an effective mentoring relationship should be. Some of my best mentors didn't sugarcoat their criticism of me. What was valuable to me was the input they gave, not the relationship per se.

I remember another one of my early professional mentors, the late Ed Doherty. Ed was a great person and a splendid writer. Once he gave me an assignment, and I turned in what I thought was a first-rate job. Doherty called me into his office. "What nationality are you?" he asked. "American," I said. "Oh, I'm sure you have deep roots in another culture," he said. Proud of my German-Irish heritage, I told him he was right. Doherty smiled and said, "Well, that explains why you can't yet write English." I was mortified. Doherty then sat me down and took me through what I had written word by word. Later he bought me *Modern English Usage* by Fowler, *The Elements of Style* by E. B. White, and Roget's *Thesaurus*. I will never forget Ed Doherty— and what he did for me in those moments when I was full of myself.

A mentor's oldest role has probably been socialization. As young people entered the workforce or started their own business, they needed to learn how to act in that particular environment. Mentors would tell them not to wear a plaid jacket to work, not to talk about business at a company social function, and to be deferential to everyone. If the protégé was an entrepreneur, the socialization process might include education about things that are part of the en-trepreneurial culture: keeping a low profile with clients, not complain-ing about anything, and not letting nonentrepreneurs know that self-employment isn't always all that wonderful.

Another benefit of mentoring is having a role model. Soap opera star Lilly Melgar found it in her mother.[5] I found it in my dad. Some find it in their first boss. Others might find it in what Martin Yate calls "virtual mentors": a character from history such as Benjamin Franklin, or a person they'll probably never meet such as actress Jodie Foster. You can "consult" your virtual mentors whenever you have a question about your behavior.[6] For instance, you might "ask" Jodie Foster what she would do if she were a victim of sexual discrimina-tion, then you would project and think about what Foster might answer. First Lady Hillary Rodham Clinton's virtual mentor is Eleanor Roosevelt.

A third benefit of mentoring can be candid advice about what to do in order to succeed, including acquiring new skills. Your mentor may tell you, for example, not to kill yourself doing reports for your boss, because the boss has little power and no one else is going to see the reports; instead spend more of your time learning about finance.

A fourth benefit is protection. As you try to increase your power and influence, mentors use *their* power and influence to keep your enemies and competitors from attacking you. This is a biggie. Without protection, many successful people wouldn't have been able to expand their turf or their business.

A fifth benefit is promotion, or sponsoring. Mentors can pave the way for your advancement. If there's a vice presidency open, they can lobby so that you'll get it. In a sense, mentors can be your public relations agents. They can talk you up to all the right people. And if they have the power, they will actually pull the strings so that you advance. Mentors have even been known to create jobs for their protégés.

Other benefits that mentors may sometimes provide are emotional support, a sense of belonging, and a chance to ventilate. But don't count on it. With the work environment now so chaotic, some of the "soft" parts of mentoring have been tossed overboard, and many such relationships have become much more straightforward.

WHAT'S IN IT FOR THE MENTOR?

What are the benefits to mentors? Well, there is the satisfaction Walter Seifert discussed. Mentoring usually makes the mentor feel a sense of accomplishment.

Also, there is frequently the expectation in many fields that professionals, as they mature or become successful, will pass on what they know to others. Those others don't necessarily have to be younger than they; an overnight success who's only twenty-four would still be expected to share know-how with recipients who might be in their fifties. People who don't participate in this ritual of passing expertise on are open to censure that they're "all get and no give."

In addition, there is usually some prestige associated with mentoring. If your protégé turns out to make it big time, your status may be enhanced.

Another benefit is the reciprocal help that protégés can sometimes offer mentors. Part of that help is in terms of information; the protégé can be the eyes and ears of the mentor. Another form of help could be sharing resources. For instance, mentors might not have the technical expertise the protégé has.

Another benefit to you as a mentor is that your protégés can increase your sphere of influence. Having a protégé in marketing, and another two in finance, can extend your tentacles throughout the organization.

THE DOWNSIDE

There are a number of potential drawbacks in the mentor-protégé relationship, too. They include:

A mismatch. The magazine *Working Woman* uses the case of Carol Bartz, who was chairman and chief executive officer of a software company. Bartz found that she had often chosen the wrong role model, something that cost her time and brought on stress. She finally realized she couldn't use any one person as a role model but should mix and match the qualities of several people.[7]

I've seen a number of cases in which young people came to L.A. or New York from another part of the country. They didn't know the lay of the land and tried to get their bearings by imitating someone who seemed to personify L.A. or New York to them. More often than not their choice was inappropriate, and the protégés wound up trying to force-fit themselves into their environment.

Lost confidence. A recent article in *Inc.* magazine described how veteran entrepreneur Ric Leichtung sent several pages of single-spaced typed criticism to junior entrepreneur Steve Leveen. Leichtung criticized Leveen's promotional material. Leveen felt the criticism was right on the money, and Leichtung became his mentor.

But the story might not have had such a happy ending. I know a woman who went from a nonprofit to the private sector. A well-meaning woman at the corporation tried to help her adjust. Unfortunately, the barrage of advice from the would-be mentor undermined the woman's confidence in her own ability to read or decode an environment. It's fifteen years later, and I don't think this woman has recovered yet. Too much input was delivered too quickly—and with no "sandwich," i.e., no praise surrounding and softening the criticism.

Overdependency. You never want to depend on your mentor too much. Mentors are supposed to be a bridge to what you want, not a Big Daddy or an Earth Mother. I vividly remember a woman in graduate school who came from an inferior college. She was lost at Ohio State and not doing well. Then her thesis adviser "adopted" her.

She blossomed, and her grades got much better. But she couldn't—or didn't want to—break the hold the professor had on her. She evolved into a mini-version of him.

The worst thing about becoming too dependent on a mentor is that you stunt your own growth. I advise young people who are in such a relationship to get out—but get out nicely. You don't want an enemy on your hands.

Guilt by association. Your mentor may lose power, may retire, may screw up. And that could reflect on you. Smart protégés avoid this sort of situation by not becoming too closely identified with one mentor. Instead, they maintain a number of mentors in the organization. Political alliances always involve political risk.

Speeding ahead of the mentor. It happens. Your mentor is a director, and then you're appointed to be senior director or vice president. There could be hard feelings. This is best handled ahead of time, while the promotion is still in the works. Discuss with your mentors the benefits that could come to them from this promotion for you. Outgrowing your mentors is a common occurrence. Your focus has to be on not injuring the mentor's feelings.

Betrayal. It's not unusual for mentors—or protégés—to feel betrayed. Maybe you perceive they're not promoting you enough. Maybe they judge that you're being too independent. This is a toughie. Perception is perception. In many cases the relationship isn't salvageable. The best you can do in such a case is defuse some of the negative feelings and continue to treat the mentor with respect.

Despite all the pitfalls, I'm convinced that it's better to have a mentor than to not have one. The best advice I could give you is to be alert for changes in the relationship. But how do you get a relationship going? There are a number of ways.

GETTING A MENTOR

In "Asking Someone to Be Your Mentor," Stephen Pollan and Mark Levine recommend that you take the initiative—but make that person think he or she is choosing you, rather than the other way around. Bring up the issue. Find common ground. Mention how much you enjoyed working with this person on a task force, or how much you were able to learn from this person's weekly presentations. If the person begs off, saying, "I don't have time," drop it and look for someone else. People who don't have time for you aren't the kinds of mentors you need.[8]

Another way to get a mentor is to go to an organization that already has a mentoring program in place. In an article in *Nation's Business*, Howard Rothman described a formal mentoring program at a $7.8-million company, Fu Associates. The *boss* does the mentoring.[9] In fact, when it comes to finding a mentor, perhaps the most overlooked resource is the boss. Especially if you want a diversified political base, your boss should be one of your mentors. (You'll also want to choose others from throughout the company, of course.) Usually you don't need to ask the boss to accept this role. If the chemistry is right, it will happen naturally.

WHAT MENTORS WANT IN A PROTÉGÉ

In *The Mentor Connection*, Michael Zey looks at this issue from the mentor's point of view. Zey interviewed a number of executives and asked what they looked for in a protégé. What makes a protégé appropriate and valuable to a mentor? Zey lists ten qualities:

- Intelligence
- Ambition
- Willingness—and ability—to deal with power and risk
- Ability to perform the mentor's job
- Loyalty
- Sharing the mentor's perceptions about the organization and work
- Dedication to the company
- Political smarts
- Positive perception of the company
- Ability to form alliances[10]

From these ten qualities, we can construct the profile of the ideal protégé.

- You are bright and alert enough to pick up on what's happening in the global economy, the industry, the organization, and the department, but not so full of yourself that you feel you have all the answers.

- You have enough desire to get ahead to be able to understand the mentor's ambition and be willing to make sacrifices to advance it.
- You exhibit enough leadership to reassure the mentor that you can make decisions and implement them, even when all the facts aren't in.
- You can jump in and take over the mentor's entire job responsibilities if necessary.
- You can tell the good guys from the bad guys.
- You share the same value system as the mentor.
- You believe in the company.
- You know how to get things done in an organization.
- You understand how to put deals together.

Less-than-ideal protégés still manage to get mentors every day. But the closer you can come to the ideal, the better may be your chance of linking up with a mentor who has influence and power.

Things to Remember

- There's no fixed definition of what a mentor is "supposed" to be.
- The protégé-mentor relationship is mutually useful.
- Beware the pitfalls of being a protégé.
- Mentors have certain qualities in mind when they select protégés.

15

MOVING ON

This chapter is must reading IF:

- You want to change jobs but aren't sure it's a good move
- Your organization has family-friendly policies, but you still get those looks when you leave at 5 P.M.
- You don't feel you're learning on the job
- You're bored

In *Money*, Karen Hube states that you'll be changing jobs five times in your career. That's 25 percent more often than workers changed jobs only as recently as 1990. And you'll be staying at each job only about eight years, as opposed to eleven years in 1990.[1]

This means that *five times*, in your working life you'll go through the gut-wrenching experience of leaving your job. So get ready. In this chapter, my aim is to help ease that transition.

MY JOB CHANGE STORY

A number of years ago I received an attractive job offer from Bob Malott, the chairman of FMC in Chicago—and one of *Fortune's* "Toughest Bosses in America." At the time I was doing very well at a large public relations agency in New York. I was constantly hopping on planes to help clients all over the globe, and I felt like a big cheese. Well, Malott made me feel even bigger. He was a wonderful guy, and

I got the impression that he thought I could walk on water. I accepted his offer, without much thought. I was to report to work September 1.

Slowly it dawned on me that I had made a big mistake. At FMC I would have only one client—FMC—whereas in the agency business I had multiple clients and lots of action. And I realized I wasn't ready to trade in New York for Chicago. My angst became so bad that I got up the nerve to call Bob Malott and ask to be let off the hook. Fortunately, Bob was a gentleman about it. He even wished me good luck.

Lesson learned: Changing jobs *should* be a tough decision. If it isn't, you're not asking yourself the right questions. I never did something dumb like that again.

A very able young man named Dwight worked for me. Dwight had a great history of success in everything he did. But it was clear that, no matter how hard he tried or how much he did, he could never be really successful in the public relations business. He didn't have a good feel for marketing. I called him in and told him that he could stay with us, but it would be better for him if he moved on. And I told him why. He protested. He told me he wanted the job and could do well. Frankly, he was scared. Well, Dwight spent two more years with us. It was wasted time. He shouldn't have done it. He did fine for us, but he didn't do fine for himself. Lesson: Don't be scared to move on if, in your heart, you know it's right.

John Johnstone, former chairman and chief executive officer of Olin Corporation, left jobs twice. One was a job he had had for twenty-three years. The other was the chairmanship of Olin. Both were hard decisions.

* * *

INTERVIEW: JOHN JOHNSTONE

RLD: What's leaving a job all about?

JJ: Well, you don't wake up some morning and say, "The hell with it," and look for another job. And you don't blame the boss. Sure, you might have a "bad" boss in the sense that the person isn't a good manager. But I've had two "bad" bosses, and I learned a tremendous amount from both of them. Unless you feel utterly trapped, a "bad" boss is no reason to rush off and leave a job. Whatever is happening, give it time to play out. Leaving a job is a serious decision and shouldn't be done without a lot of thought.

RLD: What should you consider when you're thinking about a job change?

JJ: You consider the balance between what you're learning and what you're contributing on the job. Ideally, that balance should be fifty-fifty. When you're new to a job you're learning a great deal and contributing little. If that keeps up, you're going to be out of a job. On the other hand, maybe you're one of those people who does everything right. As a result you find yourself contributing more than you're learning. So you get bored. That's how trouble starts in a career. Some organizations have recognized this and are enriching jobs—that is, they're putting more content in a job so that the person can learn more. That approach alleviates some of the frustration that occurs at organizations where there's no longer a lot of upward mobility. If it works, many of the formerly bored decide not to leave their job and stay with the organization. If it doesn't work, though, workers *will* start thinking about leaving. In short, a sense that you're no longer growing is a valid reason for leaving a job.

Another valid reason is your personal life. Is the job interfering, let's say, with your marriage? I always put my marriage ahead of the job.

These are some of the issues to consider when you're contemplating leaving your job. You should take this process slowly.

RLD: What do you mean, "take this process slowly"?

JJ: Well, after twenty-three years with one organization I didn't just run out and see headhunters and shout from the rooftops that I was available. First, I had to resolve a number of questions before I could go forward with my job search. For instance, I had to ask myself, "Do I want to work for a competitor?" I decided that after working so many years side by side with such fine people, I simply couldn't work for a competitor. Since the competition was the only appropriate place to go if I wanted a good job, I decided to start a completely different career in another industry.

And when I was chairman at Olin, I had to first "sell" to the board of directors that I wanted to retire and that I had a feasible succession plan established. I also had to do some "internal" work. I knew that I had to prepare myself for the transition from chairman to ordinary citizen. I got help there from a friend who gave me Jeffrey Sonnenfeld's *The Hero's Farewell: What Happens When the CEO Retires*. That book brilliantly captures how easy it is to try to hang onto the CEO lifestyle even after you vacate the position. It's a sad book, but useful reading for anyone who's trapped in the professional past.

The point is: It takes time to get where you *must* be in order to handle the next step, and the step after that, in your job search. A job search should never be rushed.

RLD: Is there a sign or red flag that says to you, "Time to hit the road, Jack"?

JJ: One red flag is the situation in which—for a period of time—you've repeatedly attempted to accomplish a major objective, and you're blocked. At this point, I think you have to ask yourself, "Am I in the right place?" In my mind, this is a valid reason for you and the organization to part company.

RLD: But isn't it possible to fool yourself into thinking you have an excellent reason for leaving your job? What's the moment of truth?

JJ: That moment of truth happens in the morning, when you're putting on your cosmetics or starting to shave. You look at yourself in the mirror and you ask yourself, "Did I learn anything yesterday?" Or, "Did I contribute anything yesterday?" You have to reach inside yourself and find out if you're still growing. And that all goes back to balance. If your learning and your contributing are out of balance, you have a problem.

Many bright people find a way around that. They reach outside the boundaries of their job and find new things to learn. One way to do that is to volunteer for teams. Every time you learn something new, you establish a good base for new types of contributions. Theoretically, your contribution becomes better as a result of the learning process.

RLD: How do you search for another job discreetly?

JJ: I didn't search. I was lucky. Offers came to me. But if young people are going to go the resumé-and-networking route, then it's going to be hard to be discreet—that is, if you look in your own industry. If you look outside your industry, there's less chance your job search will be uncovered.

If you're searching in your own industry, you have to prepare for the possibility that someone will say, "Hey, I understand you're looking for a job." Basically your response has to be, "I'm trying to look outside and determine what's available." Then you describe how you're not learning or contributing enough, whatever the situation is. That gives you a chance to talk about your role in the organization.

RLD: When you embark on a job search, what should your mindset or attitude be?

JJ: Organized. You have to know what your skills are—and aren't. You must know what you can do—and what you can't do. You have to know what you like to do—and not to do. Once you have all these items in the right columns, you can calmly go about a search.

RLD: Suppose your leaving isn't voluntary?

JJ: Don't panic. First of all, let me say that in most organization-initiated terminations the people let go aren't surprised. They knew that they weren't contributing enough.

Okay, the ax falls. What's next? Well, you will have to proceed more quickly than a job searcher who still has a job. But that doesn't mean you are supposed to run out and line up twelve lunches so you can network. If you move too quickly, you're going to wind up all stressed out.

Instead of rushing around, what you should do is calm down, sit down and ask yourself, "Who are the people I know? Who among them would I like to tell about this change in my circumstances?" If you have a few weeks left on the job, it's wiser for you to use that time to reflect rather than to mail out a bunch of resumés. No job search should be instantaneous. There are too many things you have to resolve in your mind first.

RLD: How do you leave an organization on good terms?

JJ: That has a lot to do with what your behavior was while you were on that job. If you didn't manage yourself well on the job, then your departure will probably not go too well. I've had good people leave Olin, and I wished them the best of luck; I knew they would have had to wait five or six years before getting a comparable position at Olin. Your superiors and coworkers usually have a good understanding of why you're leaving. And if you've been a good corporate citizen, you'll be treated with respect.

RLD: Is it possible to mend fences before you leave?

JJ: Yes, if that's what you want to do. But how well you can patch things up will depend on how well you behaved over the long haul. The act of leaving isn't that significant. What is significant is how you behaved during the five years you were at Organization XYZ.

Also, you can mend fences after you leave. Two or three months down the road you can call former bosses or colleagues, offer to buy them lunch, bring them up to date on things. Frequently, if you take that kind of initiative, you can get past some awkward parts of the relationship.

RLD: Some young people tell me that me that they move on to a new job and are disappointed. Why does that happen?

JJ: Two reasons. You panicked and grabbed just any job. And/or you didn't do the proper research on the job, the organization, and the industry.

RLD: What should young people do if they get into this sort of mess?

JJ: If you feel you're in the wrong job or the wrong organization, then stop and reflect a little. Ask yourself, "What are the chances of this getting better? Is this an organization where I want to be for the long term?"

What's critical here is the fit. Is the way the organization operates a good fit for me? Are the people here a good fit for me? If the answer is no, you can consider some alternatives. You can slowly start looking for a job. Sometimes that's wiser than hanging on for a year and being miserable; the agony shows. Or you can go to human resources and check out what else is available. You'll land on your feet as long as you don't panic.

RLD: Okay, you go on to your new job and love it. But you feel bitter about the previous job. What should you do?

JJ: We all have to talk our way through that. You need a friend, colleague, or mentor to listen to you.

* * *

NO PERFECT JOBS

John Johnstone certainly makes the point that there are valid and not so valid reasons for leaving your current job. One of the most invalid reasons I've encountered is the desire for a "perfect" job. Somewhere, for some reason, some unfortunate people have conjured up the idea that the perfect job exists. In the work world, the perfect job is a very self-destructive fantasy that leads to great discontent and job hopping. And job hopping can burn you out faster than a grueling job will. Trust me: There is no such thing as the perfect job.

William J. Kirby, senior vice president of FMC (the company I almost made a bad job-hopping move to), warns young people not to fall into the trap of believing that a new boss, more money, or a different type of organization will create that perfect job for you. The grass is rarely greener on the other side—it's just different. The closest you'll come to the perfect job is one that's a good fit for you. Focus on the fit, not on some imaginary criteria for what a perfect job should be.

Among the personal issues that should determine that fit and, in my view, take precedence over the job are the organization's family-friendly policies. An organization that proclaims it has family-friendly policies and then gives dirty looks to mothers and fathers who leave at 5 P.M. is an organization to consider leaving.

I once interviewed for a job with a major fashion organization. The pay package was great. I would have reported directly to the CEO and had a large budget and millions of dollars of foundation money to give away. But a few days before I had to make my decision, one of the people in the organization bragged to me that he had electronically bugged his coworkers' offices and found out every little tidbit on them. I politely said no to the organization and have never mentioned that story until this book. For me, such an invasion of privacy—and an organizational culture that seemed to tolerate it—was reason enough not to move on to this particular organization.

EMPLOYABILITY

Harvard business professor Rosabeth Moss Kanter uses the word "employability" in the same sense as John Johnstone uses "learning."

In *When Giants Learn to Dance*, Kanter defines "employability" as the ability to make *today's* work applicable to *future* opportunities.[2]

If you're not acquiring new skills while you're working, as Johnstone has emphasized, that's a valid reason for leaving a job. There are freelance writers and consultants who will not accept an assignment that cannot be leveraged for future business.

Also, before you take any job—at least if the organization is public—you should retrieve analysts' reports on American Online or CompuServe. Is the organization healthy, or is it troubled? Savvy people who are considering troubled organizations usually request some type of premium for taking on that risk.

GOODBYE TO THAT JOB

Switching from your present job to one that—at least in your eyes— is better is often the cause for euphoria. That could be a bad reaction, says executive search consultant Robert Half. In "Leaving a Job," Half advises you not to "gloat to others about the new and wonderful job to which you are going." He sees that as "overplaying your triumph in getting a new position."[3]

Gloating is unwise because, first of all, you're setting up a me-against-them dichotomy. There you are, going off to this wonderful job, while all those poor slobs are trapped in their jobs in the same old company. Second, it's inappropriate because—implicitly—you're challenging the left-behinds to get some initiative and get a good job just like yours. Third, you might not be smiling for long. In *What Your Boss Can't Tell You*, Kent Straat warns, "Don't underestimate the value of your investment in your current position." At the old job you have the organizational culture, the products, and the idiosyncrasies of the players all down cold.[4] In the new job, you may not ever be able to acquire the same knowledge base—and even if you can, it will take plenty of time. The adjustment to your new job may be so difficult that you'd like to seek out the familiar—that is, people you know from the old job. Don't alienate them during the goodbyes.

EXIT INTERVIEWS

Another sensitive issue is exit interviews. They're not confidential. Therefore, use your common sense. You don't want to say anything during an exit interview that could hurt your own good name or make you appear to be a crybaby. The purpose of the exit interview is to provide information to the organization about why people leave. More money, more responsibility, a shorter commute—all are conventionally acceptable reasons why you're leaving your job. Exit interviews were not created to be a form of therapy in which you can ventilate your feelings about how the bosses and your colleagues did you wrong. Deliver that tirade into a tape recorder and listen to how bad it sounds.

I always encourage young people to write a constructive letter on the way out. It helps everyone.

BENEFITS AND COMPENSATION

Other important items you have to handle are your benefits and compensation. In an article entitled "Your Worklife" in *Money* magazine, Karen Hube stressed that you *must* square away these items before you leave the company. "Once you close the door, don't count on anyone arranging extended benefits or pay," says Hube.[5]

Find out when your health care benefits become effective on the new job (human resources can tell you that). If there's a gap—perhaps your new benefits don't go into effect for several months—you can use your current benefits in the interim. Yes, even if you quit, you can extend your benefits! The federal COBRA law allows you to extend your current coverage at group rates. That way you'll pay less than you would on an individual policy. If you don't sign up for COBRA, you can still be covered for sixty days if you pay the premiums retroactively. This means, in other words, that you don't have to stay in the old job just to hold on to your health care.

If you're close to being vested in the organization's pension plan, it might be financially worth your while to hang in there a little longer. That way you'll get both your pension contribution and your employer's contribution. The wise thing—though not always the possible thing—is not to touch this nest egg. You can roll the whole thing over into your new employer's retirement plan or into an Individual Retirement Account (IRA). Consider consulting a financial planner about this.

You may have vacation days due you. If it's not yet bonus time, can you get a portion of that bonus when you leave, or will you receive the whole thing when the other bonuses are given out?

YOU'RE IN CHARGE

In the new economy, you're in charge of your career. This chapter just presents guidelines. What's important is for *you* to take charge. In *How to Make the Right Career Moves*, Deborah Perlmutter Bloch counsels against passivity. For example, she sees the "I wish they would fire me" attitude as too passive a stand. If you think it's time for you to move on, you have to be the one to initiate the move.[6]

Things to Remember

- A job change is a serious decision.
- There are valid and invalid reasons for a job change.
- You're responsible for your own career.

CONCLUSION

This chapter is must reading IF:

- You want to continue to be successful
- Everything around you keeps changing

Congratulations. You now know the ropes. You can graduate from boot camp. You can go out there and get what you want. You understand everything that it took my generation and myself 14 years to learn.

ALL ABOUT STRATEGY

Oh, you'll forget a lot of the details you read about in this book. For example, you probably won't remember some of the characters on the grapevine such as the Good Mother. And you've probably already forgotten how many times entrepreneurs fail before succeeding. But what you should have down cold is that in your professional life you have to think strategically. Your career, your professional reputation, your promotions and pay raises—they're all about strategy.

For instance, you just don't access the grapevine in your office and start asking about Joe. Before you approach the grapevine you should have thought through: (a) Why are you asking about Joe? (b) Whom are you approaching to ask about Joe? (c) What will this information about Joe "cost" you in terms of favors you'll owe? (d) What happens if Joe finds out that you've been asking about him? Every one of your actions in work has a multiplicity of consequences. That's what you have to think about before you act.

You won't be successful, at least not for long, if you don't approach every aspect of your professional life on a strategic basis. That ranges from whom you get to be friends with at work to how you manage your bosses when they have personal problems.

Smart pros—those who win in the workplace—think of their career as a business they're running. It's as important to them as Microsoft is to Bill Gates. You would be wise to approach your professional life in the same manner. That means that you ought to be objective. If something is hurting the business, then you have to look at that factor in your life. Suppose the computer-sciences degree you're going for at night is making you irritable during the day. People are noticing. What do you need to do about that? You're working in White Plains, New York. You feel out of the loop and aren't meeting many colleagues from Manhattan. What are your options? You checked with headhunters, and your compensation is below the average. Is that any way to run a business? What do you want to do about that?

You can no longer depend on the company or boss to look out for you. Your career is now entirely your business.

STRATEGIC PLANNING MEETINGS

At least once a week you must have a "strategic planning meeting" about your business. You can conduct those meetings alone, by yourself. Or you can invite your mentor or friends to attend. You want to analyze where you've made progress that week and what your setbacks were. Are your original goals becoming outdated? For instance, maybe your goal was to become assistant manager in two years. Your organization has started to downsize. Maybe your new goal should be to survive for the time being or to hunt for another position in a more secure environment. Another aspect of the business to keep looking at is your contacts. Is your circle getting bigger or smaller, and what are the quality of those contacts? In your inner circle should be some people who challenge you and push you to be your best professional self. What new skills have you been learning? Are you bored?

BEING HAPPY

In your strategic planning sessions you also have to look at the emotional part of your life. Are you happy? Your happiness is as important to your success as the MBA you picked up or the new product you're working on in the design studio. Happy people, whether in organizations or self-employed, tend to get ahead.

At a telecommunications organization there was a man I'll call John. John did not have one of those profiles for big success. He wasn't a tall, good-looking WASP. His ethnic origin officially classified him as a minority, and in those days members of his ethnic group were not exactly on the fast track at any organization. John's education was also atypical. He hadn't gone to a brand-name college full-time; instead, he had attended a local college in the evening. He started his career with the organization in a blue-collar position, and it is usually difficult, almost impossible, to move from blue collar to white collar. Yet John rose, seemingly effortlessly, to the upper tiers of the organization. Despite plenty of reorganizations, John is still there. And still walking the halls with a smile.

Over the years, we John-watchers analyzed his rise to leadership positions. We had to agree that John was no tiger like GE's Jack Welch. He wasn't brilliant, not in any particular area of business. His energy level was average. And, on his watch, mistakes had been made. So there were blemishes on his track record.

We came to attribute John's professional success to the fact that he was a happy person. People liked being around him. Since he wasn't bursting with resentments against the world and the organization, there was no chance that he would lash out at you. He was rarely if ever suspicious that various factions were out to get him; that made him seem relaxed and intelligent. If attacked at a meeting, he calmly explained the facts. He seemed to see no percentage in carrying a grudge. The people who worked for John loved him. Most of his superiors were interested in his doing well, so they would help him over the rough spots. John thrived. And is still thriving.

Go into your local department store and observe the young people who work at the counters. Some of them are happy doing what they're doing—at least for the time being—and some are not. Some are full of self-pity and will tell you, "I went to University X, and here I am, a clerk in retail." I predict that those unhappy people won't move from that counter. The happy people, on the other hand, make a good impression on you. You enjoy doing business with them. Some of those happy people will be selected by the store to be buyers and managers. Some of them will take the initiative to enroll in the Fashion Institute of Technology or take some business courses. Some might open their own store. For the unhappy people there's usually nowhere to move; they're blocked by their unhappiness.

If you're not happy at work, find out why. And do something about it. Maybe you're in the wrong work environment. Maybe you're in the wrong profession. Maybe you're simply in the wrong city; you should be in L.A. instead of New York. The longer you're unhappy at work, the more your professional reputation will suffer. Unhappiness shows. And because it does, it has always been a career killer.

THE FIVE GOALS

In your strategic planning sessions you want to review the five goals we spoke about in the Introduction. Those five goals should be the "pull" force in your career. If you're not making progress toward those goals, your career is probably stalled.

Self-knowledge

Self-knowledge is a moving target. As circumstances change, you will probably change, and you might have to get acquainted with yourself all over again. When I left corporate life and became an entrepreneur, I changed. I had to take the time to figure out who I was, what my priorities were, and what sacrifices I was willing to make for the business. My relationship with my wife also changed. For instance, I could no longer guarantee her a regular paycheck. My relationship with my children changed. I had to consider whether the risks I was taking in my own business would hurt them. For instance, if I took a risk in dealing with Client X, and Client X dropped me and went to another agency, did that mean the children wouldn't be going to Disney World that year?

Every week, write down the ten things that are most important to you in work. Then write down the ten things that are most important in your personal life. Those lists should change over time. If they don't, either you're not growing or you don't know who you are.

Empathy

Whether you're firing a subordinate or congratulating a boss on her success, you have to assess how that person feels. If you can walk in that person's shoes, you will be successful in your career—and avoid those interpersonal disasters that sideline many a competent professional.

You learn empathy by being in close touch with how you yourself feel. Suppose your boss just received a promotion. Conventional wisdom would have it that she should be elated. From your own experience with success, though, you know that a new victory can stir up a lot of old self-doubts. So you might want to reassure the boss that she's up to the new challenge. Be heavy on the reassurance and lighter on the praise.

If you lack empathy, you're going to make plenty of interpersonal mistakes. They always create havoc. You tell the person who just got laid off how bad the job market is. You tell the person who just got made assistant manager how much resentment there is about the promotion. You tell the secretary how bright he is and how he should get an education to get a better job. Eventually you're going to get kicked out of the organization or lose your business.

Once a week, check out how you're feeling about things. If you're feeling that way, many in your professional circles probably have similar feelings.

Presenting Yourself

Often people make judgments about you based on very little information. No one understands this better than salespeople. Salespeople who make cold calls know that their fate rests on their voice. If their voice doesn't immediately hit the person called the right way, they're in trouble.

Professionally you present yourself on the phone, on paper, in person, online, and in front of groups. How you present yourself in the workplace when you first get out of college should be different from how you present yourself when you're promoted to director. One of the biggest mistakes young people make is not realizing that they have to change their image. As you get more confidence, for instance, you could become more low-key, less eager to please.

When you don't reconfigure your image at the appropriate times, there's a discontinuity. There you are, a manager of marketing, presenting yourself like a cheerleader in high school. You will find that people will treat you as you appear, not according to your official rank in the hierarchy. There are so many Rodney Dangerfields—who get no respect—in organizations because so few people recognize that they have to readjust their image as their circumstances change.

Every month look at yourself in the mirror. Look over your clothes in the closet. Does what you see represent who you are now? Listen to your voice in a tape recorder. Do you overexplain things? Do you still sound like a kid, or is there authority in your voice? What's your body language saying about who you are?

Being Informed

Your fourth goal is to stay informed. That encompasses everything from keeping current with the information on the grapevine to knowing how to surf the Internet.

In the current work world, deficits in knowledge will be held against you. The boss gets annoyed that you can't read a balance sheet. Shouldn't you have known that this was knowledge needed to do your job?

Ask superiors and colleagues what you should be learning. Notice what skills your colleagues have that you should acquire. If the majority of your peers are certified in insurance, maybe you should also become certified.

Every month, take an inventory of your skills and knowledge base. Compare those with your peers in your department and other organizations. You might find that you are so far ahead of your colleagues that you could probably earn significantly more money in another organization.

Problem Solving

Your mantra should be, "Don't bring bosses problems, bring them solutions." In the organization or in your own business you want a reputation as a problem-solver. Very capable professionals hurt their image because they get overwhelmed by problems. Instead of just solving the problems, they talk about and confess their doubts that they can find solutions. They wind up shaking other people's confidence in them.

Every week, review the problems in your personal and professional life. Ask yourself, "What would a top-notch problem solver do about these difficulties?" Some young people who are problem-phobic ask themselves, "What would a normal person do in this situation?" And the immature among us can ask themselves, "What would an adult do about those problems?"

Then judge if it's time to begin to implement a solution. Timing can be everything. Solving a problem just to get it out of the way can produce disasters. There was a young man who really wanted a divorce. So he applied for one immediately—when he was between jobs. He wound up in financial hell. After you solve the problem, ask yourself how you might solve similar problems better in the future. Experience should make you a better problem solver.

YOUR PLAYING FIELD

Whether you have your own business or work for someone else, it's your playing field. That's because it's your decision where and how you are going to earn a living. If those choices don't work out, you're going to have to find the courage to make some changes. No matter how exciting your business or job is, you're not going to work all the time. Successful people who remain successful have balance in their lives. And you're going to care about how happy you are.

Your career is truly yours.

Things to Remember

- Career success means strategic thinking.
- Happiness is a factor in success.
- Pay attention to knowing yourself, empathy, presenting yourself, information, and problem solving.

NOTES

Introduction

1. Daniel Goleman, *Emotional Intelligence* (New York: Bantam Books, 1995), 43.

Chapter 1: Good Professional Fits, Bad Professional Fits

1. John Kotter and James Heskett, *Corporate Culture and Performance* (New York: Macmillan, 1992), 11.
2. David Drennan, *Transforming Company Culture* (London: McGraw-Hill, 1992), 1.
3. Ibid., 3.
4. James Collins and Jerry Porras, *Built to Last* (New York: Harper Business, 1994), 89.
5. Edgar Schein, *Organizational Culture and Leadership*, 2d ed. (San Francisco: Jossey-Bass Publishers, 1992), 8–10.

Chapter 2: Getting Inside

1. Robert Wegman, Robert Chapman, and Miriam Joseph, *Work In The New Economy* (Indianapolis, Indiana: JIST Works and New York: American Association for Counseling and Development, 1989), 89.
2. Martin Yate, *Beat The Odds* (New York: Ballantine Books, 1995), 45.
3. Charles Handy, *Age of Unreason* (Boston: Harvard Business School Press, 1989), 237.
4. U.S. Bureau of Labor Statistics as quoted in *Industry Week*, June 3, 1996, 44.
5. Law School Admission Council as quoted in *U.S. News & World Report*, April 1, 1996, 44–49.
6. Brad Johnson, *Restaurants & Institutions*, March 1, 1996, 120–25.
7. Howard Isenberg, *Management Accounting*, October 1993, 54.
8. Robert Adams, ed., *The Adams Cover Letter Almanac* (Holbrook, MA: Adams Publishing, 1995), passim.
9. Roger Ailes, *You are the Message* (New York: Doubleday, 1988), 1–3.

10. Wegman, Chapman, and Joseph, *Work in the New Economy*, 89–93.

Chapter 3: On Your Own

1. Steven Bursten, *The Bootstrap Entrepreneur* (Nashville, TN: Thomas Nelson Publishers, 1993), 25.
2. John Case, "The Dark Side: Births and Deaths," *Inc.*, May 15, 1996, 80.
3. Ibid.
4. Jeff Porten, *The Twentysomething Guide to Creative Self-employment* (Rocklin, CA: Prima Publishing, 1996).
5. Ibid., 1, 3.
6. Arthur A. Thompson Jr., *Economics of the Firm*, 2d ed. (Englewood Cliffs, NJ: Prentice Hall, 1977), 257.
7. Fred Bleakley, "Many Firms See Gains of Cost-Cutting Over, Push to Lift Revenues," *Wall Street Journal*, July 5, 1996, 1.
8. Karen Abarbanel, *How to Succeed on Your Own* (New York: Henry Holt, 1994), 1.
9. Ibid., 12–16.
10. Irving Burstiner, *The Small Business Handbook* (New York: Simon & Schuster, 1994), 54–61.
11. Gustav Berle, *SBA Answer Book* (New York: John Wiley & Sons, 1992), 1.
12. William Alarid and Gustave Berle, *Free Help From Uncle Sam to Start Your Own Business (or Expand the One You Have)*, 3d ed. (Santa Maria, CA: Puma Publishing, 1992).
13. Philip Lader, "SBA Update," *Entrepreneur*, June 1996, 110.
14. Lynn Beresford, "Bon Appetit," *Entrepreneur*, June 1996, 95.
15. Kristin Dunlap Godsey, "Sharp Antenna," *Success*, August 1996, 12.

Chapter 4: You and Your Bosses

1. Michael Verespej, "Workers Rate Their Bosses," *Industry Week*, August 3, 1992, 31–32.
2. Kenneth Labich, "Brutal Bosses and Their Prey," *Fortune*, March 18, 1996, 23.
3. "Blame the Bosses," *Small Business Reports*, July 1993, 26.
4. "Dithers in the '90s," *Forbes*, March 11, 1996, 21.
5. John Gabarro and John Kotter, "Managing Your Boss," *People: Managing Your Most Important Asset* (Cambridge, MA: Harvard Business Review, 1988), 1–9.
6. Fleming Meeks and Dana Wechsler, "Trickle-down Bosses," *Forbes*, November 7, 1994, 206.

7. Mardy Grothe and Peter Wylie, *Problem Bosses* (New York: Facts on File Publications, 1987), 21–39.

8. Steve Blickstein, *Across the Board*, April 1994, 31–36.

9. Robert Carey, "Coming Around to 360-degree Feedback," *Sales & Marketing Management*, March 1995, 56–61.

10. Gabarro and Kotter, 3.

11. Daniel Goleman, *Emotional Intelligence* (New York: Bantam Books, 1995), 96.

Chapter 5: Working the Grapevine

1. "Did You Hear It Through the Grapevine?" *Training & Development*, October 1994, 20.

2. Terrence Deal and Allan Kennedy, *Corporate Cultures* (Reading, MA: Addison-Wesley, 1982), 85.

3. Keith Davis, "Management Communication and the Grapevine," *People: Managing Your Most Important Resource* (Boston: Harvard Business Review, 1988), 85.

4. Gordon Allport and Leo Postman, *The Psychology of Rumor* (New York: Henry Holt, 1947), 75.

5. Davis, 85.

Chapter 6: Networking

1. "Mr. Creativity," *The Economist*, August 17, 1996, 55.

2. Jessica Lipnack and Jeffrey Stamps, "Networking the World," *Futurist*, July–August 1993, 9.

3. Diane Cole and Loraine Calvacca, "Getting Your Names on Everybody's Lips," *Working Woman*, August 1989, 68.

4. "Networking 101: Seeing and Being Seen," *Nation's Business*, March 1966, 11.

5. Andrew Olson, "Long-term Networking," *Management Review*, April 1994, 34.

6. Mickey Veich, "Networking for Success," *Security Management*, September 1994, 32–36.

7. Landy Chase, "Networking," *American Salesman*, December 1994, 16–23.

8. Veich, 32–36.

Chapter 7: Making Allies of Baby Boomers

1. Suneel Ratan, "Why Baby Busters Hate Baby Boomers," *Fortune*, October 4, 1993, 56–57.

2. Diane Crispell, "When Generations Divide: A Guide," *American Demographics*, May 1993, 9–10.

3. Bruce Tulgan, *Managing Generation X* (Santa Monica, CA: Merritt Publishing, 1995), 22.

4. Karen Ritchie, *Marketing to Generation X* (New York: Lexington Books, 1995), 16.

5. Rosabeth Moss Kanter, *When Giants Learn to Dance* (New York: Simon & Schuster, 1989), 328.

6. Richie, passim.

7. Ratan, 57.

8. Wayne Johnson, "Move Over Rover, Let Jimi Take Over: But Will He Ever Get Out of the Way," *Air Conditioning, Heating, & Refrigerator News*, May 20, 1996, 18.

9. Michael Hammer, *Beyond Reengineering* (New York: Harper Business, 1996), 49.

Chapter 8: Image

1. Roger Ailes, *You Are the Message* (New York: Currency, 1988), passim.

2. Edward Valdez and Kim Valdez, "The Professional Makeover: Tips for Reengineering Your Image," *Hispanic*, January–February 1995, 98.

3. Charles Fombrun, *Reputation* (Boston: Harvard Business School Press, 1996), 72–73.

4. Susan Bixler, *The Professional Image* (New York: G P. Putnam's Sons, 1984), 31.

Chapter 9: Having Influence at Any Level

1. "Time's 25 Most Influential Americans," *Time*, June 17, 1996.

2. Ibid., 81.

3. Allan Cohen and David Bradford, *Influence Without Authority* (New York: John Wiley & Sons, 1991), 17–19.

4. Leonard Marcus, "Negotiating to Shift Power Without Losing Influence," *American Medical News*, March 4, 1996, 37.

5. Ian Pierce, "Power and Influence's Role in Communications," *Communication World*, March 1996, 7–8.

6. Jeffrey Pfeffer, *Managing With Power* (Boston: Harvard Business School Press, 1992), 216.

7. Robert Cialdini, *Influence: The Psychology of Persuasion* (New York: William Morrow, 1984), 17–56, 57–113, 114–66, 167–207, 208-36, 237–72.

8. Robert Dilenschneider, *Power and Influence* (New York: Prentice Hall, 1990), 11–18.

9. Cialdini, 21–23.

10. Pfeffer, 209.

11. Cialdini, 173.

12. Daniel Goleman, *Emotional Intelligence* (New York: Bantam Books, 1995), 97.

Chapter 10: School

1. Russell Jacoby, *Dogmatic Wisdom* (New York: Doubleday, 1994), xiv.

2. Mel Elfin, "The High Cost of Higher Education," *U.S. News & World Report*, September 16, 1996, 90–95.

3. Viva Hardigg, "Full House at Film School," *U.S. News & World Report*, March 21, 1994, 94–95.

4. "Social Science and the Citizen: Costs and Benefits of Higher Education," *Society*, Jan.–Feb. 1993, 2.

Chapter 11: Your Work and Your Personal Life

1. William Whyte, Jr. *Organization Man* (New York: Simon & Schuster, 1956), 146.

2. Julia Lawlor, "Bottom Line on Work-Family Programs," *Working Woman*, July–August 1996, 54–59.

3. Ibid., 54–59.

4. Harris Collingwood, "Surprise: Men Use Work-Family Benefits, Too," *Working Woman*, February 1996, 15.

5. Lawlor, 54–59.

6. Jill Smolowe, "The Stalled Revolution," *Time*, May 6, 1996, 1.

7. "Mother's Day Is Every Day," *Business Wire*, May 9, 1996, passim.

8. Lisa Jenner, "Work-Family Programs," *HR Focus*, January 1994, 19–20.

9. "Merck Ranks Tops for Working Moms, *Working Mothers* magazine," *Business Wire*, September 10, 1995, 9.

10. "The Benefits Trailblazers," *Direct*, March 1993, 40–43.

11. Lawlor, 54–59.

12. Ibid.

13. Smolowe, 63.

Chapter 12: The Right Thing to Do

1. John Marks, "The American Uncivil Wars," *U.S. News & World Report*, April 22, 1996, 70.

2. Tim Carvell, "Crabs With Miss Manners," *Fortune*, September 9, 1996, 44–46.

3. Cheryl Jarvis, "Prescribing Good Manners," *Nation's Business*, May 1994, 18.

4. Marks, 72.

5. Marjabelle Young Stewart, *Executive Etiquette in the New Workplace* (New York: St. Martin's Press, 1994), 12.

6. Barbara Pachter and Marjorie Brody, *The Complete Business Etiquette Handbook* (Englewood Cliffs, NJ: Prentice Hall, 1995), 16–17.

7. Jan Yager, *Business Protocol* (New York: John Wiley & Sons, 1991). Letitia Baldrige, *Letitia Baldrige's New Complete Guide to Executive Manners* (New York: Rawson Associates, 1993).

8. J. R. Bradstrander, "Naughty or Nice," *Barron's*, December 11, 1995, 38.

9. Dana Nigro, "Manners Matter," *Meetings & Conventions*, June 1995, 76–79.

10. Julie Conelly, "Have We Become Mad Dogs in the Office?" *Fortune*, November 28, 1994, 197–99.

11. Ibid.

12. Pachter and Brody, 37.

13. Ibid., 219.

Chapter 13: After a Setback

1. Michael Barrier, "Back From the Brink," *Nation's Business*, September 1995, 18–23.

2. Robert James, *Churchill: A Study in Failure* (New York: World Publishing, 1970), passim.

3. John Lord, *Song of the Phoenix: The Hidden Rewards of Failure* (Stockbridge, MA: Berkshire House, 1992), 50.

4. Neil Steinberg, *Complete and Utter Failure* (New York: Doubleday Dell, 1994), 4.

5. Karen Richie, *Marketing to Generation X* (New York: Lexington Books, 1995), 40–43.

6. Gilbert Brim, *Ambition: How We Manage Success and Failure Throughout Our Lives* (New York: Basic Books, 1992), 61.

7. Lord, 43–63.

Chapter 14: Mentors

1. Joshua Adams, "My Mentor, Myself," *Town & Country Monthly*, August 1994, 60–68.

2. Michael Zey, *The Mentor Connection* (Homewood, IL: Dow Jones–Irwin, 1984), 6.

3. Kathy Kolbe, "Avoiding a Mentor Mismatch," *Working Woman*, October 1994, 66–68.

4. Zey, 7.

5. Ann Kirchheimer, "Like Mother, Like Daughter," *Hispanic*, January–February 1995, 28–30.

6. Martin Yate, *Beat the Odds* (New York: Ballantine Books, 1995), 137.

7. Kolbe, 66–68.

8. Stephen Pollan and Mark Levine, "Asking Someone to Be Your Mentor," *Working Woman*, August 1995, 53.

9. Howard Rotham, "The Boss as Mentor," *Nation's Business*, April 1993, 66–68.

10. Zey, 1982.

Chapter 15: Moving On

1. Karen Hube, "Your Worklife," *Money*, November 1995, 41.

2. Rosabeth Moss Kanter, *When Giants Learn to Dance* (New York: Simon & Schuster, 1989), 321.

3. Robert Half, "Leaving a Job," *Management Accounting*, November 1991, 14.

4. Kent Straat, *What Your Boss Can't Tell You* (New York: American Management Association, 1988), 266.

5. Hube, 41.

6. Deborah Perlmutter Bloch, *How to Make the Right Career Moves* (Chicago: NTC Publishing Group, 1990), 70.

FOR FURTHER READING

Chapter 1: Good Professional Fits, Bad Professional Fits

Deal, Terrence, and Kennedy, Allan. *Corporate Cultures*. New York: Addison-Wesley, 1982.
Sculley, John. *Odyssey*, New York: Harper & Row, 1987.

Chapter 2: Getting Inside

Shechtman, Morris. *Working Without a Net*, Englewood Cliffs, NJ: Prentice Hall, 1994.
Tepper, Ron. *Power Resumés*, 2d ed., New York: John Wiley & Sons, 1992.
Washington, Tom. *Resumé Power*. Bellevue, WA: Mount Vernon Press, 1990.

Chapter 3: On Your Own

Drucker, Peter. *Innovation and Entrepreneurship*. New York: Harper & Row, 1985.
Kern, Coralee Smith, and Wolfgram, Tammara Hoffman. *How To Run Your Own Home Business*. Lincolnwood, IL: NTC Publishing Group, 1995.
Kishel, Gregory, and Kishel, Patricia Gunter. *How to Start, Run, and Stay in Business*. 2d ed. New York: John Wiley & Sons, 1993.
Mancuso, Joseph. *How to Start, Finance, and Manage Your Own Business*. New York: Random House, 1993.
Sexton, Donald, and Kasarda, John, eds. *The State of the Art of Entrepreneurship*. Boston: PWS-Kent Publishing, 1992.

Chapter 4: You and Your Bosses

Bolton, Robert, and Bolton, Dorothy Grover. *People Styles at Work*. New York: American Management Association, 1996.
Forsyth, Donelson, *Group Dynamics*. 2d ed. Pacific Grove, CA: Brooks/Cole Publishing, 1990.

Chapter 5: Working the Grapevine

Pfeffer, Jeffrey. *Managing With Power*. Cambridge, MA: Harvard Business School Press, 1992.

Chapter 6: Networking

Hadley, Joyce, and Sheldon, Betsy. *The Smart Woman's Guide to Networking*. Franklin Lakes, NJ: Career Press, 1995.
Roane, Susan. *How to Work a Room*, New York: Warner Books, 1988.

Chapter 7: Making Allies of Baby Boomers

Dunn, William. *The Baby Bust*. Ithaca, NY: American Demographics Books, 1993.
Light, Paul. *Baby Boomers*. New York: W. W. Norton, 1988.

Chapter 8: Image

Adatto, Kiku. *Picture Perfect*. New York: HarperCollins, 1993.
Leinberger, Paul, and Tucker, Bruce. *The New Individualists: The Generation After The Organization Man*. New York: HarperCollins, 1991.

Chapter 9: Having Influence at Any Level

Dawson, Roger. *Secrets of Power Persuasion*. Englewood Cliffs, NJ: Prentice Hall, 1992.

Chapter 10: School

Bloom, Allan. *The Closing of the American Mind*. New York: Simon & Schuster, 1987.
Drucker, Peter. *The New Realities*. New York: Harper & Row, 1989.
Rossman, Mark. *Negotiating Graduate School*. Thousand Oaks, CA: Sage Publications, 1995.

Chapter 11: Your Work and Your Personal Life

Covey, Stephen. *The Seven Habits of Highly Effective People*. New York: Simon & Schuster Fireside Books, 1990.
Miller, Timothy. *How to Want What You Have*. New York: Avon Books, 1995.
Schwartz, Tony. *What Really Matters*. New York: Bantam Books, 1995.

Chapter 12: The Right Thing to Do

Darling, Jan. *Outclassing the Competition*. New York: St. Martin's Press, 1985.

Chapter 13: After a Setback

Corson, William R. *Consequences of Failure*. New York: W. W. Norton, 1974.
Sterns, Ann. *Coming Back: Rebuilding Lives After Crisis and Loss*. New York: Random House, 1988.

Chapter 14: Mentors

Bernstein, Charles. "Stuart Levin: Mentor to Hundreds" *Restaurants & Institutions*, February 1, 1995, 48.
Kupfer, David. "What's the Best Advice You've Ever Been Given by a Leader or Mentor?" *Whole Earth Review*, Winter 1995, 68–70.
Regins, Belle Rose, and Cotton, John. "Gender and Willingness to Mentor in Organizations." *Journal of Management*, Spring 1993, 97–102.
Turner, Allison. "Mentor Program Introduces Students to Life in Real Business World." *South Florida Business Journal*, July 22, 1994, 15A–17.

Chapter 15: Moving On

Kleiman, Carole. "Changing Jobs for the Right Reasons." *Des Moines Register*, February 11, 1996.
Krannich, Ronald. *Change Your Job, Change Your Life*. Manassas Park, VA: Impact Publications, 1995.
Snelling, Robert, Sr. *The Right Job*. New York: Penguin Books, 1993.

INDEX